# AUDITING REIMAGINED

# AUDITING REIMAGINED

Navigating Stakeholder Expectations

BY

**YUSUF M. SIDANI**
*American University of Beirut, Lebanon*

**TAREK EL MASRI**
*Prince Mohammed Bin Salman College of Business & Entrepreneurship, Saudi Arabia*

AND

**ABDELJALIL GHANEM**
*American University of Beirut, Lebanon*

United Kingdom – North America – Japan
India – Malaysia – China

Emerald Publishing Limited
Emerald Publishing, Floor 5, Northspring, 21-23 Wellington Street,
Leeds LS1 4DL.

First edition 2025

Copyright © 2025 Yusuf M. Sidani, Tarek El Masri, and Abdeljalil Ghanem.
Published under exclusive licence by Emerald Publishing Limited.

The content of this publication has not been approved by the United
Nations and does not reflect the views of the United Nations or its
officials or Member States. For more information on the United
Nations Sustainable Development Goals see: https://www.un.org/
sustainabledevelopment/sustainable-development-goals/.

**Reprints and permissions service**
Contact: www.copyright.com

No part of this book may be reproduced, stored in a retrieval system,
transmitted in any form or by any means electronic, mechanical,
photocopying, recording or otherwise without either the prior written
permission of the publisher or a licence permitting restricted copying
issued in the UK by The Copyright Licensing Agency and in the USA
by The Copyright Clearance Center. No responsibility is accepted
for the accuracy of information contained in the text, illustrations
or advertisements. The opinions expressed in these chapters are not
necessarily those of the Author or the publisher.

**British Library Cataloguing in Publication Data**
A catalogue record for this book is available from the British Library

ISBN: 978-1-83708-667-2 (Print)
ISBN: 978-1-83708-664-1 (Online)
ISBN: 978-1-83708-666-5 (Epub)

INVESTOR IN PEOPLE

*To auditors who dare reimagining their profession*

# CONTENTS

*Preface* xiii
*Yusuf M. Sidani*

1. The Evolution and Challenges of the Auditing Profession 1
   Auditing History 3
      Medieval Auditing Practices 5
      Growth of the Profession 6
      The 20th Century and On 9
   Challenges 12
      Fraud Detection 13
      Talent Attraction and Retention 15
      Oligarchy 19
      Auditor Independence 21
   Conclusion 24
2. What Stakeholders Want: Understanding the Audit Expectations Gap 25
   The Expectations Gap 27
   Drivers of the Expectations Gap 32
      Self-regulation and Professional Evolution 32
      Performance Deficiencies 34
      Standards and Regulatory Frameworks 35
      Public Perceptions and the Expectations Gap 36
   Outcomes of the Expectations Gap 37
      Increased Litigation Risk 37

|   |   |   |
|---|---|---|
| | Conflicts at Various Levels | 37 |
| | Lobbying and Overregulation | 38 |
| | Impact on Reputation and Credibility | 39 |
| | Conclusion | 39 |
| 3. | Auditing: From Professionalization to Commercialization | 41 |
| | What Organizational Cultures? | 43 |
| | Professional Logics Versus Market Logics | 46 |
| | Professional Logics | 47 |
| | Commercial Logics | 48 |
| | Legitimizing Commercialization | 52 |
| | Identity | 55 |
| | The Accountant Identity | 56 |
| | Identity and Professionalism | 57 |
| | Risks of Stereotype Shifts | 57 |
| | Identity Crises and Reconstruction | 59 |
| | Conclusion | 59 |
| 4. | Institutional Inertia and Institutional Entrepreneurship in Auditing | 61 |
| | Factors Contributing to Institutional Inertia | 61 |
| | Behavioral Inertia and Path Dependence | 62 |
| | Resistance to Change and the Status Quo | 63 |
| | The Impact of Scandals and Self-regulation | 64 |
| | Lobbying and Regulatory Influence | 64 |
| | Embracing a New Mindset in Auditing | 65 |
| | The Role of Institutional Entrepreneurship | 66 |
| | The Role of Big Accounting Firms | 66 |
| | A Return to Professionalism | 67 |
| | Identity Reconstruction | 68 |
| | Evolution of the Professional Accountant's Image | 68 |

|  |  |  |
|---|---|---|
| | The Role of Institutional Entrepreneurs | 69 |
| | Changing the Accounting Stereotype | 69 |
| | Redefining Auditing | 70 |
| | Embracing Change in the Audit Profession | 70 |
| | Addressing Auditor Responsibilities in Fraud Detection | 71 |
| | The Shift Toward Real-time Auditing | 71 |
| | Expanding Assurance Services Beyond Financial Information | 72 |
| | Leveraging Technology for Comprehensive Audits | 73 |
| | Adapting to New Accounting Principles | 73 |
| | Overcoming Institutional Inertia | 74 |
| | Conclusion | 74 |
| 5. | Bridging the Gap: Reimagining Auditing for the Future | 77 |
| | ACE: The Future Auditor, Agile, Competent, and Ethical | 79 |
| | A: Agility | 79 |
| | C: Competence | 79 |
| | E: Ethical Grounding & Character | 80 |
| | PLACE: Educational Institutions – Schools of Business | 80 |
| | P: Professional Development | 81 |
| | L: Leadership Skills | 82 |
| | A: Alignment with Industry | 82 |
| | C: Character & Ethics Development | 82 |
| | E: Experiential & Lifelong Learning | 83 |
| | EMBRACE – The Profession (Ethical Practice, Mentorship, Building Relationships, Responsiveness, Acceptance, Communication, Excellence) | 83 |
| | E: Ethical Practice | 83 |
| | M: Mentorship | 84 |
| | B: Building Relationships | 84 |

| | |
|---|---|
| R: Responsiveness | 84 |
| A: Acceptance | 85 |
| C: Communication | 85 |
| E: Excellence | 86 |
| Conclusion | 86 |
| *About the Authors* | 89 |
| *References* | 91 |
| *Index* | 121 |

Critics of the auditors are right in two respects: that the industry matters, and that it needs reform. It is in everyone's interest that auditing works.

*The Economist. (2018a)*

# PREFACE
## Yusuf M. Sidani

Early in my professional career, I knew an experienced auditor, whom I'll call Ryan, who was still working well beyond his retirement age. Charismatic, eloquent, and impressive, Ryan often shared stories about his experiences as an auditor. As an inexperienced young auditor, I found his stories to be more insightful and inspiring than any "fundamentals of auditing course" could offer. Stories inform and inspire, and his certainly did.

One of the many stories I heard from him, more than once, was about a difficult judicial investigation he faced while auditing a failing company in an Asian country. The investigator questioned him about an alleged fraud, inquiring why the auditor "could not uncover the fraud before it happened and why he waited till it happened before reporting it." To fully grasp the seriousness of the discussion, one had to listen attentively to Ryan, as he always conveyed it with a hint of sarcasm. "When he asked me this question, I responded by asking why the police do not uncover crimes before they happen." Things went downhill from there, and it was only by luck that Ryan was not detained on the spot.

To be fair to the investigator, one might interpret his question as asking why the auditor didn't institute precautionary measures or monitor the internal controls needed to prevent the fraud. However, Ryan could clearly see that the entire case stemmed from misunderstandings and unmet expectations, as well as misinterpretations about the real role of an auditor. Is an auditor a gatekeeper, a watchdog, a police officer, an insurer against fraud, a compliance enforcer, or some type of co-manager?

Upon hearing more about the case, one would understand the irony. The auditor had been formally appointed only a few weeks earlier and had visited the company just once. Ryan noted, "They were still decorating the offices, and I couldn't detect any business activity happening at the time." His team had not started their audit procedures, except for the typical requests for documentation, trial balances, and other information in preparation for the fieldwork. The auditor had not issued any report or communication and was not expected to do so for some time.

Yet, the auditor found himself and his firm in the middle of a judicial investigation and facing the threat of disciplinary action. It took many more months of investigations and judicial work, along with a different understanding of the auditor's role and responsibility by another investigator within the judicial system, for Ryan and his firm to be acquitted.

It was not only a matter of misunderstanding what Ryan did or did not do at the time. In the grand scheme of things, this was also about unmet expectations. We expect the auditor to alert us to fraud or potential fraud, to include a large enough sample in their work to uncover errors and irregularities, and to protect us as shareholders, potential investors, or other users of the financial statements. While these expectations are often reasonable, there are cases where they are not.

These latter cases might include instances where an auditor diligently performed their duties, assigning their best personnel to the audit, properly planning the audit process, and allocating the necessary time and resources for its execution. Despite this, there is no guarantee that every error will be uncovered or that nothing will go wrong. After all, an audit opinion provides "reasonable" assurance, not absolute or complete assurance. This level of assurance is often not sufficient for someone who has lost their investments due to reliance on the audit report.

The audit profession has been struggling with a persistent issue where what people expect from auditors does not match what auditors actually deliver, thus creating a gap in expectations that does not seem to go away. Despite significant advancements in accounting and auditing standards, educational approaches, auditor training, and technology, this gap persists. This ongoing issue has been harming the profession. Every year, millions of flawless audits are carried out, but it only takes a few hundred cases around the globe – or even less – to tarnish a profession that has long prided itself on its professionalism and prestigious social status.

The reasons for this gap, as explained in this book, are myriad. Some reasons pertain to unreasonable societal expectations, ignorance about the real role of auditors, deficient standards, and even unfair media attention that often puts auditors in a negative light. Yet, in many cases of corporate failure, the reason might be more germane to the profession itself. Sometimes, the problems relate to a profession that has failed to evolve or be responsive enough, leaving itself in a state of inertia.

We address some of these issues in this book, reflecting on the history and performance of a profession that is in dire need of transformation. Our hope is that the profession can reinvent itself and reimagine its role to reaffirm its vital role in the functioning of societies and economies around the world.

# 1

# THE EVOLUTION AND CHALLENGES OF THE AUDITING PROFESSION

*To win back the public trust, audit faces the challenge of re-envisaging its service through its primary purpose*

*(Buddery et al., 2014)*

On New Year's Eve in 2018, a federal judge in Alabama found that one of the Big Four accounting firms had failed to uncover a long-standing fraud, citing this as professional negligence: "the case has sent shockwaves through a profession that has long sought to limit its responsibility for detecting malfeasance" (Masters, 2018). Despite industry lawyers expressing their anger over the ruling, the case concluded with a $335 million settlement between the Federal Deposit Insurance Corporation (FDIC) as Receiver for Colonial Bank and the auditing company, down from the $625 million initially ordered by the court (FDIC, 2019).

Holding an external auditor liable for not uncovering fraud is a common occurrence. To many in the auditing profession, this ruling was outrageous, failing to consider the auditor's role and the limitations clearly expressed in audit reports. Conversely, some observers contend that we should hold auditors accountable for their failure to detect major fraud schemes. Many users of financial statements rely on auditors for their decisions, making it unacceptable for auditors to fail in their expected duties.

Such incidents highlight an expectations gap where audit practitioners and other users disagree on the role of auditors. Several corporate fiascos over the years, linked to audit failures, have not helped the auditors' case. The auditing profession faces several challenges, including a persistent disparity between auditors and other stakeholders regarding their expected duties. These challenges also include an increase in corporate failures partially attributed to auditors, purported conflicts of interest, the impossibility of audit independence (Bazerman et al., 1997), and challenges brought about by digital transformation. Additionally, challenges arise in the education of future auditors, which have a significant impact on higher education institutions. This has led to multiple calls for audit and accounting reforms and initiatives at professional, regulatory, and educational levels to address these issues. In this book, we reflect on these challenges and how they operate in different contexts and regulatory frameworks.

The audit expectations gap is a significant and persistent challenge for the audit profession. This gap is now "worse than ever," noted an accountant with 40 years of experience in a letter to the *Financial Times* (Akther & Xu, 2020; Kingsley, 2018). Many stakeholders accuse auditors of failing to meet expectations, which leads to decline in trust in the auditing profession (Oliver, 2018) and increased perceptions that auditors are not performing their jobs properly, resulting in accusations of professional negligence (Coram & Wang, 2021). Audit committees, board members, investors, creditors, regulatory authorities, and others have become increasingly demanding of auditors (PTI, 2018). This has resulted in calls to redefine auditor roles (Mackie, 2018), hence transforming the auditing profession itself (Kelly, 2018). This is particularly important given the ongoing evolution of the accounting and auditing professions, driven by newer standards, technological advancements, and many other factors, which have in many cases compounded the expectations gap (Holtzman, 2004).

Multiple studies have confirmed the existence of a gap. The Cohen Commission of Auditors, as early as 1978, sought to determine "whether a gap may exist between what the public expects or needs and what auditors can and should reasonably expect to accomplish" (Cohen Commission, 1978, p. xi). The Commission identified an expectations gap and urged audit professionals and other parties involved in the preparation and presentation of financial statements to work together to bridge it. Despite repeated attempts by the auditing profession to close the gap, it has persisted. This has led to calls to examine this phenomenon, investigate its implications, its drivers, and how the profession should address it (Izza, 2019).

This book evaluates various understandings of the expectations gap, with a focus on the role of the auditing profession. Earlier reviews (e.g., Ali et al., 2015; Chye Koh & Woo, 1998; Omodero & Okafor, 2020) have not focused on the role of the audit profession and how institutional forces influencing the profession contribute to the persistence of the expectations gap. Understanding these factors can help identify what impedes substantial change. We argue that the auditing profession suffers from institutional inertia, which dilutes genuine industry restructuring to confront the audit expectations gap. We stress the importance of institutional entrepreneurs in breaking down this inertia and argue that the audit profession needs to play a significant and proactive role in addressing it, as it is best positioned to do so. We conclude by emphasizing the need for an innovative mindset in the auditing profession, necessitating a reimagining of the profession's role and a reconstruction of the auditor's identity.

Before exploring these issues, we provide a brief overview of the evolution of the audit industry. The profession today is vastly different from its past; the perception of a professional auditor now is not the same as it was many decades ago. Understanding the profession's history and transformations is crucial for envisioning its future path and opportunities.

## AUDITING HISTORY

The word "audit" originates from the Latin word "*audire*," which means "to hear." This reflects the practice of early auditors, who would listen to verbal clarifications and explanations about the state of accounts from managers. Various sources indicate that forms of accounting and auditing existed in Ancient Egypt, Ancient Greece, the Roman Empire, and the nascent Muslim empire (Meuwissen, 2014).

Auditing is considered one of the "most ancient of all professions. Early civilizations apparently learned to audit almost as soon as they learned to write" (Smolinski et al., 1992, p. 7). Early tablets show writings by inspectors counting agricultural products. Other discoveries indicate that a form of auditing existed in ancient Mesopotamia, Egypt, Greece, and Rome. In ancient Athens, a basic form of audit included a system of accountability for public funds (Lane, 2023; Woolf, 1912), and public officials were subject to record examinations by government auditors (Atkinson & Jones, 2014, p. 329).

A culture of accounting flourished during the Roman era (LaGroue, 2014), with auditing functions aimed at preventing potential fraud by quaestors. Quaestors were individuals tasked with supervising the state treasury, and auditing was part of their roles (Kesimli et al., 2019). After leaving office, they were required to submit their accounts for examination by the newly appointed quaestors and also by the Roman Senate (Smolinski et al., 1992).

Some scholars note that a form of auditing over public finances existed in the early Islamic era. One of the pillars of Islam, *Zakat*, involved the collection of alms for the benefit of special categories of the poor, needy, and other authorized expenditures. This process required developing a function for collecting and disbursing these funds, along with monitoring and accountability mechanisms. Omar Ibn El Khattab, the second Caliph, established an administrative unit known as the *dewan*. The *dewan*, literally translating to "office" or "bureau," managed and monitored the state budget and oversaw public expenditures. One of these bureaus, the Bureau of *Beit-ul-Mal* (treasury), was responsible for monitoring collections and expenditures.

Associated with the development of these bureaus was the institution of *hisbah*, or "accountability." Guided by the Islamic principle of promoting good and forbidding evil in the marketplace, this historical institution involved appointing a *muhtasib*. This role loosely corresponded to an early form of auditing and market monitoring, ensuring that merchants followed proper practices in their transactions (Dogarawa, 2013; Rasyid, 2013; Talar, 2012; Zakiyah et al., 2019).

Although the *muhtasib's* role was broad and included non-financial aspects, the economic aspect was significant in ensuring legal and ethical practices. The role included fraud prevention and oversight of pricing mechanisms. Some responsibilities encompassed the broader notion of operational audit, such as ensuring product quality and inspecting production and merchandise. The *muhtasib's* role is similar to an auditor's in another respect: reporting any wrongdoing in market practices to the authorities (Attahiru et al., 2016), which is akin to contemporary auditors reporting issues to relevant stakeholders in their audit reports.

## Medieval Auditing Practices

Medieval times saw the emergence of more formal states, necessitating the development of an accountability system for the collection of taxes owed to the ruling classes. This necessitated the development of record-keeping and accountability systems. In medieval England, particularly under Henry I (1069-1135) and Henry II (1133-1189), an effective and strong state emerged, reinforced by a relatively efficient financial system (Jones, 2008). This period saw the need for financial controls, leading to the emergence of an early model of auditing. This was triggered to ensure accountability regarding state revenues and the financial affairs of various entities linked to the state, including religious institutions (Jones, 2008). One example of an audit mechanism that emerged was the exchequer audit, introduced by Henry I and further developed by Henry II, to manage the collection of royal revenue from the English shires. The system involved the adoption of written records and an audit. Understandably, this audit was primitive compared to the modern professional role, neither comprehensive nor methodical (Jones, 2009).

Woolf (1912) reports that in the 13th century, Leonardo Fibonacci, a well-known writer in Italy, was tasked with auditing the accounts of a certain commune. As trade networks evolved, ruling elites found more ways to accumulate wealth (Smieliauskas et al., 2020). With the growth of state powers and wealth accumulation came the need for accounting systems to measure revenues and wealth, and accountability systems to monitor the accuracy of record-keeping and limit fraud.

Two key milestones advanced accountability tools: the development of Arabic numerals and the double-entry bookkeeping system.

These developments improved the tracking of various accounts, culminating in the double-entry accounting system by Pacioli in 1494 (Smieliauskas et al., 2020, pp. 9–10). Pacioli's bookkeeping method spread across Europe, facilitating record keeping and profit determination. This greatly advanced the formation of accounting science and the gradual development of financial and cost accounting methodologies for better-informed decision-making. With better accounting methodologies came the need for improved accountability and auditing mechanisms.

By the 17th century, the notion of a "professional auditor," a role occupied by a trained person, was established (Woolf, 1912). LaGroue (2014) explained how early audit practices emerged in England and Scotland during the 16th and 17th centuries, focusing on validating and verifying the accuracy of accounting records. Auditors were tasked with ensuring the correctness of account entries, as highlighted in the 1564 English Book of Ordinances. Due to the expansion of bankruptcy laws in the late 17th century, auditors increasingly addressed legal requirements. This trend intensified in the late 18th century, particularly after the loss of the American colonies, when many entities and individuals faced significant financial losses or bankruptcies. The role of an auditor evolved, reflecting the increasing complexity of business operations, legal frameworks, and the onset of the Industrial Revolution (LaGroue, 2014).

## Growth of the Profession

At the dawn of the industrial revolution, businesses began to grow, and their operations and structures became more complex. This increased the need for a better understanding of accounting and the accuracy of accounting records, triggering a demand for more formalized and standardized auditing processes and a professional auditing field. As businesses started to include outside investors who did not participate in daily operations, the need to provide an accurate picture and protect their interests grew in parallel. The profession transformed from a simple record-keeping system into one essential for advancing accountability and fraud detection (AbdulGaniyy, 2013).

The modern auditing profession emerged in Britain during the first half of the 19th century, driven by the growth of industrial activities and regulatory requirements. In 1831, a bankruptcy act provided the first "public recognition" of accountants as skilled professionals capable of conducting audits (ICAEW, n.d.). The UK Companies Act of 1844 mandated that directors of public companies maintain records and have their accounts verified by independent auditors, marking an early formal use of fair presentation. This legislation built on longstanding practices, and by the mid-1800s, early accounting firms that represent the precursors of the modern profession were established: Samuel Lowell Price (1849), William Deloitte (1845), William Cooper (1854), and William Barclay Peat (1870) (Meuwissen, 2014). The American Association of Public Accountants was founded in 1887, and it represented the first collective effort to garner national support and recognition in the USA (King & Case, 2016). In 1917, it became the American Institute of Accountants, later changing to its current name, the American Institute of Certified Public Accountants (AICPA), in 1957.

Around the 1850s, in Scotland, accountants operated within the legal profession, establishing a collaborative relationship with lawyers. During this time, the accountancy profession continued to grow. However, it became clear that the existing auditing system lacked methodological rigor, effective audit procedures, and professional independence. There was a growing realization of the importance of an independent auditing function:

*In 1860, John Hollingshead complained about the inadequate, if not incompetent, auditing practices of joint-stock companies. Only when company managers and shareholders are compelled to 'call in professional accountants and resort to an independent investigation' will real auditing become a necessary part of a business organization, and the longer it is neglected, the more costly it becomes (quoted in Schmitt et al., 2002).*

During the Victorian era, auditors sought to verify each transaction (AbdulGaniyy, 2013), a practice that later evolved into a sampling approach. The Victorian age saw the emergence of new professions alongside traditional ones like lawyers and medical doctors, including engineers and accountants (Lee, 2011). Professionals began to organize into associations, signaling increased professionalization across these sectors. This era witnessed a shift from pre-capitalist values, such as a sense of "calling" and duty to community, to a market-oriented approach (Larson, 1977; Lee, 2011). The establishment of the Institute of Chartered Accountants in England and Wales (ICAEW) in 1880 was a critical juncture in the development of accounting. This occurred through the merger of five existing accounting organizations in response to growing industrial developments and business complexity.

By the end of the 19th century, professional auditors increasingly conducted financial statement audits. British firms established offices in the USA, driven by British businesses starting operations there. This significantly contributed to the development of the American accounting and auditing professions, with the first U.S. national accounting firm founded in 1883. The Certified Public Accountant (CPA) designation began in New York in 1896 and later spread to other states (Smieliauskas et al., 2020). The designation of "chartered accountant" was introduced in Scotland in 1854, followed by England and Wales in 1880. In the USA, the New York Stock Exchange mandated periodic financial reporting around 1899 (Smieliauskas et al., 2020), enhancing the relevance of professional auditing services.

The auditing profession established its identity during this era. At that time, there was no universally accepted framework for professional auditors and no general acceptance of the boundaries of their roles and responsibilities. The judiciary's role in interpreting auditors' obligations and duties further complicated this matter, leading to several legal cases reflecting early signs of an expectations gap. The Kingston Cotton Mill decision was ultimately recognized as a milestone, bringing some stability and confidence to the profession by defining, more clearly, auditors' roles and responsibilities. While these and later rulings did not entirely remedy the expectations gap, as it remains relevant today, it was during this era that modern auditing practices began to take shape with a better clarity of auditors' roles and responsibilities (Teo & Cobbin, 2005).

In 1879, based on a Companies Act in Great Britain, all banks were required to have audited accounts. In 1882, the ICAEW held its first examinations, with auditing as a topic. By 1900, all limited companies were required by a Companies Act to produce annual audited balance sheets (ICAEW, n.d.). Early audit offices were founded in Britain and then a presence was established in the USA, transferring the profession and its institutional practices (Flesher et al., 2005). It is worth noting that financial scandals that have characterized the last few decades are not new as similar scandals occurred in the late 19th century leading some to the conclusion that "audit failures in Britain are as old as auditing itself" (Matthews, 2006b).

## The 20th Century and On

The modern auditing profession saw significant developments starting with the Companies Act of 1900 in the UK, which required companies to appoint independent auditors, marking the beginning of contemporary auditing practices (Meuwissen, 2014). This act laid the groundwork for further formalization of the profession through additional regulations and standards issued by regulatory bodies.

The stock market crash of 1929 (Bierman, 2013) was a watershed event in US history, leading to the enactment of the Securities Act of 1933 and the Securities Exchange Act of 1934 and the establishment of the Securities and Exchange Commission (SEC). During earlier periods, companies would issue stocks and actively promote their potential value to motivate investors to buy, often without any substantive basis. The above acts mandated that all SEC registrants produce financial statements audited by independent auditors, greatly contributing to the positioning of the audit profession and the relevance of services offered by independent professionals (Levy, 2020). These Acts also drove the mandatory requirement for auditor appointments according to the Securities and Exchange Act of 1934 (Meuwissen, 2014). Another momentous incident toward the end of that decade was the McKesson & Robbins audit scandal, which led to an SEC investigation and the 1939 issuance of the first authoritative auditing standard (Levy, 2020).

Matthews (2006a) notes that until the 1960s, auditors often performed the dual roles of preparing financial statements and auditing. Auditors rarely conducted a "pure audit." Auditors relied, perhaps excessively, on management's assertions regarding asset valuations, with little emphasis on audit planning, sample determination, or risk assessment. However, pure audits became more frequent, and statistical methods were increasingly employed. The emphasis on balance sheet audits increased, as did the focus on internal controls and compliance. Auditors began using working papers, questionnaires, flowcharts, and audit manuals more extensively.

In 1977, The International Federation of Accountants (IFAC) was established, comprising 63 members from 51 nations. Its aim was to strengthen the global accountancy profession by issuing high-quality international standards in areas related to accounting and auditing and promoting their adoption. This was one of many steps that contributed to a global convergence over the years. Although there has been an increase in adoption, these standards have not been adopted uniformly. More recently, 160 of the 168 jurisdictions at a global level have developed a commitment to International Financial Reporting Standards (IFRS, 2023). All G20 jurisdictions have also expressed a level of commitment to IFRS Accounting Standards (IFAC, 2018a). Studies by the International Federation of Accountants have noted that about 80% of jurisdictions at a global level have adopted the International Standards for Auditing for mandatory audits (IFAC, 2018b).

The 1980s saw further advancements in audit techniques, with risk assessment and analytical reviews becoming increasingly recognized and important, reflecting a shift from transaction processing auditing to analytical and risk-focused auditing. The 1990s saw another significant transformation in the audit profession due to economic growth, globalization of business, technological advancement, increased regulatory pressures, and corporate scandals. Technology continued to revolutionize auditing practices throughout that period until the present day. The audit profession expanded its approaches by adopting technology-aided auditing and the provision of non-audit services.

The fall of Enron in 2001 and the alleged shredding of documents by employees at Arthur Andersen were milestone events for the audit industry. At the time, Arthur Andersen received about USD 25 million for auditing compared to USD 27 million in consulting fees. This revived an old debate about the impact of non-audit services on audit quality amid suspicions of conflicts of interest. The events surrounding the Enron collapse and similar corporate failures led the US Congress to pass the Sarbanes-Oxley Act of 2002. This act established the Public Company Accounting Oversight Board, marking a significant change in the audit profession. The objectives of the act included overseeing the audits of public companies subject to securities laws, setting standards and rules for audit reports, and inspecting, investigating, and enforcing compliance among registered public accounting firms, their personnel, and certified public accountants (Congress, 2002). It amended the Securities Exchange Act of 1934 in certain respects, providing guidance and additional rules regarding auditor independence. It elaborated on the role of the audit committee, called for enhanced financial disclosures, and imposed criminal penalties related to destroying or falsifying audit evidence (Congress, 2002).

In 2003, the Smith Report provided audit committees with additional guidance on auditor independence. The UK adopted the International Standards on Auditing (ISAs) in 2004, and the Financial Reporting Council (FRC) issued adapted versions known as ISAs (UK). Many initiatives have been conducted over the past 20 years to further advance audit quality, improve the profession, and restore trust in audit and corporate governance (ICAEW, n.d.).

This period also witnessed more consolidation of the audit industry from the earlier Big Eight to the Big Five and later the Big Four after the fall of Arthur Andersen. Currently, the Big Four accounting firms continue to dominate the profession. Their services now extend far beyond mere accounting and auditing, as a large portion of their revenues relates to non-audit services. They are significant in size and power, with annual revenues in the billions of dollars, and they employ nearly 1.5 million people (Bohne, 2025) across almost every nation in the world. They are also heavily involved in lobbying activities. While they are reputed for their ability to deliver complex services at a global level across various industries and contexts, their ability to consistently deliver high-quality audits has sometimes been questioned. A series of scandals and corporate failures over the years involving these firms led to heavy criticism from stakeholders, including regulators, investors, and the media. Accounting practitioners and scholars alike have highlighted the expectations gap, suggesting a disconnect between what these firms, and by extension the entire industry, offer and what the public expects them to deliver.

In sum, regulatory changes, economic conditions, financial scandals, and inter-country practices have molded the auditing profession, leading to more professionalization and development of audit practices. The last few decades have seen significant developments in the profession, including the convergence of international accounting and auditing standards, the growing power of large accounting firms, particularly the Big Four, and significant regulatory pressures aimed at bridging expectations gaps, advancing audit quality, and ensuring audit independence (FRC, 2018). There has also been a drive for greater effectiveness and efficiency in the industry, along with efforts to advance audit methodologies and approaches. This includes the growing adoption of risk-based auditing; the increased use and significance of computer-aided auditing and data analysis; and, more recently, the adoption of artificial intelligence. Tim Ryan best summarizes the current situation: "The reality is there's room for improvement in our profession, both in substance and in appearance, and there are things that we need to think about proactively" (Foley & O'Dwyer, 2023).

These transformations have presented significant opportunities for the auditing profession, impacting its economic position, reputation, and image. However, they also pose substantial challenges and raise questions about the future of the profession, which scholars, practitioners, regulators, and professional bodies continue to address.

## CHALLENGES

This rich history since ancient times has led to the development of a well-recognized profession that is vital to the world economy. Although the primary role of auditors is to provide an opinion on financial statements, their impact is much broader. The public often perceives auditors as more than just "opinion-givers"; they are seen as "watchdogs," "gatekeepers," "custodians of public trust," "guardians of financial truth," "stewards and curators of strategic information," and "protectors of investors and the public" (Martin, April 25, 2023; Ramanna, 2019; Trinkle et al., 2021; Wijaya et al., 2021). These perceptions may not match auditors' identities or what standards and regulations require. Over the years, auditors have faced numerous challenges, including discrepancies in expectations, perceived responsibility for fraud detection, commercialization of the industry, the oligarchic nature of the industry, and continuous challenges related to audit quality and auditor independence. We address some of these issues in the following sections.

## Fraud Detection

The role of auditors in detecting fraud has been a contentious issue, contributing to the gap in expectations. In the USA, regulators have been considering expanding the role of auditors to include a greater role in fraud detection (Maurer, 2024). A recent proposal by the Public Company Accounting Oversight Board (PCAOB) aimed at getting auditors to "flag possible fraud" caused a split in the vote within the board. One argument against this proposal is that it broadens the role of the auditor to become both an auditor and a fraud detector or a "guarantor against fraud"; such an expansion would fundamentally change the profession.

In a document titled *"Consideration of Fraud in a Financial Statement Audit"* (AICPA, 2023), it was noted that fraud is a legal concept and "auditors do not make legal determinations of whether fraud has occurred." Instead, auditors are concerned with actions that lead to material misstatements. The document reinforces the importance of professional skepticism, which reflects a critical mindset toward management assertions about the financial statements and the evidence provided in support of those statements. Auditors need to consider various information available to them to identify risks that can result in material misstatements. However, the document clearly states that designing effective structures and controls for the prevention, deterrence, and detection of fraud is a managerial responsibility. It reiterates the 1987 report by the Treadway Commission: "The responsibility for reliable financial reporting resides first and foremost at the corporate level. Top management, starting with the chief executive officer, sets the tone and establishes the financial reporting environment. Therefore, reducing the risk of fraudulent financial reporting must start with the reporting company." The auditor's responsibility is to plan the audit and implement procedures to obtain reasonable assurance that the financial statements are free of material misstatement, whether intentional or not. Although the audit profession commonly agrees on this, business circles have a less clear picture particularly during or after corporate failures.

Auditors face competing challenges when approaching their audit assignments, and they must balance their attention between two things (Austin, 2023). First, they must be attentive to the planned audit procedures. Second, they must be alert to the possibility of fraud. They struggle to balance the two, and one sometimes takes precedence. In a context where there is a high risk of fraud, auditors might not be able to give adequate attention to the potential for fraud while conducting the planned audit procedures. Some studies provide evidence for this phenomenon. For example, in one experimental study involving 73 auditors, Austin (2023) uncovered volatility in auditors' attention to signals of fraud during the testing stages of the audit. In sum, and in the context of audit work and uncovering fraud, auditors face a significant tension between balancing efficiency in audit work and its effectiveness. On the one hand, auditors feel the pressure of the business world and other stakeholders, who demand better audit quality and more agencies in uncovering fraud. On the other hand, they understand internal and industry pressures for efficiency and all the discourse around "auditing smarter" rather than harder (Makkawi & Schick, 2003).

A study as far back as 1977 assessed perspectives regarding the auditor's responsibility for detecting and disclosing irregularities and illegal acts (Baron et al., 1977). The authors reported significantly different beliefs held by auditors compared to non-auditors regarding the auditor's responsibility for detecting and disclosing fraudulent and illegal activities. More recent studies corroborated this phenomenon (e.g., Alleyne & Howard, 2005). Despite all of the pushback from the profession, the expectations gap regarding responsibility for fraud prevention, detection, and disclosure persists. Some make the argument that it is largely the audit profession's failure to adequately address this gap (Vanasco, 1998, p. 60): "Rather than moving toward a philosophy of a comprehensive fraud prevention, the auditing profession worldwide seems to be in a constant motion to enact statutes and auditing standards after the fraud scandals have been reported widely in the press." This criticism requires reflection on what exactly is meant by "comprehensive fraud prevention" and what that would entail in terms of audit planning and audit work.

The auditing profession has addressed considerations of fraud in audit planning and audit work. For example, the profession is aware, or needs to be aware, of the importance of understanding managerial motives for fraud in fraud risk assessment (Kassem, 2024). The ISA 240, titled *"The Auditor's Responsibilities Relating to Fraud in an Audit of Financial Statements,"* requires auditors to conduct a fraud risk assessment and maintain a degree of professional skepticism when approaching the audit. In a study relevant to this standard, Kassem (2024) conducted a series of interviews with external auditors to understand how they evaluate managerial motives for fraud. The author discovered that this assessment hinges on the auditor's critical mindset, their ability to observe managerial attitudes, their foresight in identifying fraudulent accounts, and their depth of experience in fraud examination. The challenge lies in the increasing expectations placed on auditors as they strive to enhance their expertise. The irony is that the ability to uncover fraud in one instance will invariably increase the expectation that an auditor will uncover fraud in future instances.

Reviewing the existing literature on fraud-risk assessment performance, Chui et al. (2022) note improvements due to the growing emphasis on the issue and regulatory pressures. The challenge is that as auditors are pushed to grow their expertise and actually develop it, more will be expected from them. This will raise the bar higher and higher, and no significant narrowing of the expectations gap will eventually materialize.

## Talent Attraction and Retention

Over the past few decades, attracting and retaining talent has become a significant challenge for businesses, particularly in roles requiring cognitive skills beyond physical labor (Sidani & Al Ariss, 2014). This "war for talent" deeply affects the accounting profession and is considered a persistent, long-term issue in many countries (Nouri & Parker, 2020).

Employee turnover is not new but exemplifies the intense competition between accounting firms, other industrial groups, consulting companies, and even within the firms themselves. The auditing profession, in particular, struggles to recruit and retain talent. For instance, between 2020 and 2022, over 300,000 accountants and auditors left the profession in the USA (Blood & Yong, 2024). A survey revealed that 43% of chief audit executives and audit directors are concerned about the severe consequences of insufficient talent (Flood, 2023). In other countries, contextual pressures are not helping. Brexit and migration regulations, for example, have exacerbated the skills shortage in the UK, leading to an increase in voluntary departures due to lifestyle choices (ICAEW Insights, 2023). Reflecting this need, audit companies often announce new openings. In 2023, for example, Deloitte announced plans to hire 3,000 new employees, a third of whom would be in audit and taxation (Boo, 2023).

Surveys indicate low career satisfaction among audit employees, high turnover intentions, complaints about compensation and workload, and doubts about reaching partner levels (e.g., ACRA-ACCA, 2012). Job security alone is insufficient to retain auditors (Maurer, 2023), and the requirements for certification and continuing education make it challenging to attract and keep professionals in the industry. Additionally, the perception of auditing as a high-risk occupation due to heavy regulation further deters potential talent (Tadros, 2023).

The industry faces extreme competition for talent, with "poaching" being a common practice (Yapa et al., 2017). Large firms are not immune to poaching, pushing them to stay vigilant about their talent attraction and retention strategies. For example, in June 2024, the US consulting firm Alvarez & Marsal planned to poach hundreds of key employees from the Big Four accounting firms (Foley, 2024c). This competition is even more strenuous in mid-size and smaller firms, as aspiring professionals prefer to join big names in the industry (Chen, 2024).

Audit quality, a major concern for audit firms and users of financial statements, closely correlates with the level of expertise of human resources available in audit firms. Losing employees who have received substantial training or leaving the industry altogether threatens audit firms and the quality of their audits. Research indicates a significant correlation between employee turnover and audit quality issues: "Some level of attrition is expected within audit firms. But a comparatively high rate of turnover or auditor transfer within a firm may adversely affect audit quality" (PCAOB, 2015, p. A-8). Employees who "leak" out of the firm, or out of the industry altogether, after their employers investing heavily in their training, pose a significant threat to audit firms and the quality of their audits (Künneke et al., 2017).

The profession's image of overworked and underpaid workers hampers its ability to attract top talent (Wilson, 2024). The audit profession is often a steppingstone to other jobs in the industry or consulting, making some leading accounting firms attractive first-stop career stations for young graduates before they transition into other, more lucrative positions outside the audit industry. Leading accounting firms remain excellent attraction points for young graduates who compete for positions or internships there. The influx of fresh graduates has resulted in relatively low salaries for junior auditors, an image that accounting firms often perpetuate through lower salaries and longer working hours. To counter this, the industry has been moving to highlight career opportunities and value, along with specific benefits and flexibility for aspiring professionals (Yuen et al., 2020).

Several other factors also contribute to the talent shortage in the audit industry (Mason, 2024). The rigorous demands to qualify as a professional, such as obtaining ACCA or CPA qualifications, are challenging. The skills of accounting or auditing professionals are transferable to other lucrative fields like finance, internal audit, or consulting, which often offer higher compensation and varied experiences. The auditor's image as having an investigative mindset and compliance focus is not attractive to many promising professionals. The supply of qualified graduates has declined, and the path to professional qualification is complicated, impacting economic functioning (HR Director, 2023).

The talent shortage in auditing has a ripple effect on the global economy, leading to a lack of oversight and accountability, which can result in costly fines and reputational damage for companies. This lack of confidence in the financial system can cause further economic instability. Globally, this issue is becoming increasingly prevalent, not just in American or European contexts (Blood & Yong, 2024). The fact that many talented individuals seek more exciting roles outside the audit profession leads to increased stress and workload for those who remain, resulting in burnout and reduced job satisfaction. Reports indicate rising mental health issues among audit professionals. A survey by the Association of Chartered Certified Accountants (ACCA) found that 61% of respondents identified a lack of work-life balance as a negative factor driving talent away from the audit profession (Diolas, 2024). The situation is worse among the Big Four firms, with nearly three-quarters of respondents reporting strained mental health due to work pressures, and 51% considering resignation (McCann, 2024). This situation can have significant consequences for the organization and the work culture, potentially even surpassing the act of resignation itself. Diolas (2024) highlights the following findings within the report:

> *A compelling insight from our study highlights the absence of a commonly understood and unified purpose within the audit profession. This not only inhibits prospective candidates from entering the profession in the first place, but also hinders current professionals from recognizing how their work generates value.*

Advancements in technology and AI capabilities add pressure on audit firms to hire and retain the right talent. While the need for routine accounting and audit jobs is expected to decline, the demand for skills aligned with expertise and AI is rising. To keep up with these advancements, audit firms find themselves challenged to invest further in the talent of their employees, hoping to enhance their ability to attract and retain the right professionals (Thomson Reuters Tax & Accounting, 2024a, 2024b).

The war for talent does not mean that accounting firms have an ever-increasing demand to recruit. Due to factors within the industry and contextual considerations, sometimes firms find themselves in need of laying off employees. What contributes to the phenomenon is the sensitivity of the consulting arms of accounting firms to the economic situation. Although auditing generates less revenue than consulting, the former tends to be more stable and less volatile. Revenues from consulting get a boost during phases of economic growth but tend to suffer in times of economic uncertainty (Kao, 2023).

## Oligarchy

A few firms dominate the auditing industry, generating a significant portion of the overall revenues. According to Statista (Bohne, 2024), Deloitte was the largest in 2023 with total revenues of USD 64.9 billion, followed by PwC with USD 53.09 billion, EY with USD 49.4 billion, and KPMG with USD 36.4 billion. The combined revenue of these firms exceeded USD 200 billion in 2023 and has been steadily increasing. In contrast, the next six companies combined generated about USD 45 billion. The Big Four accounting firms employed over 1,450,000 people, with Deloitte being the largest employer at 457,000 employees. The Global Data World Survey reported a fee income of USD 253.6 billion for the top 31 accountancy networks (Pickard & Naumenko, 2024), highlighting the Big Four's control of approximately 80% of total billings.

In 2023, auditing and assurance services accounted for about a third of the Big Four's revenues: Deloitte (USD 20.1 billion), PwC (USD 18.7 billion), EY (USD 15.1 billion), and KPMG (USD 12.6 billion). The immense power of these firms and their provision of non-audit services in addition to traditional audit and assurance services have raised multiple concerns, including calls for their breakup (Coffee, 2019). Many audit firms have responded with resistance. EY, for example, embarked on a project named Everest aiming to spin off the consulting and tax advisory business. The project was halted due to objections from the US arm of EY. In June 2024, the *Financial Times* reported that EY's new global chief executive ruled out any plan to split the firm into two (Foley & Foy, 2024).

Despite their immense size, power, and ability to invest heavily in improving audit processes, programs, and methodologies, the Big Four have not been immune to allegations of contributing to audit failures. The Big Four's governance issues have come under scrutiny after several such failures (Foley, 2024a). US regulators initiated "culture reviews" to assess potential organizational cultural issues contributing to these failures. Unlike multinational corporations, the Big Four and other accounting networks consist of legally separate and independent member firms, which have implications for accountability and auditor liability.

The Big Four are often seen as an oligopoly. While some authors suggest signs of deconsolidation in the audit industry (Aobdia et al., 2016), the dominance of the Big Four has long characterized the market. Mergers among large accounting firms and Arthur Andersen's exit following Enron's collapse further facilitated this trend. Increased market dominance raises concerns about audit quality, independence, and fee control (Elayan et al., 2024). In some cases, this "collective dominance" may impact audit quality and fee structures, particularly with the alleged "tacit collusion" among firms (Billard et al., 2011).

Continuous criticism facing the profession and professional audit entities, particularly regarding the role of the Big Four, has led to calls for "audit reform," increased competition, and mitigation of conflicts of interest. Opinions differ on whether decreasing the Big Four's power or fragmenting them would benefit the profession (The Economist, 2018a, 2018b).

Despite their size and reach, all Big Four firms have experienced scandals and negative media exposure due to alleged audit failures. This is especially disheartening, considering their global dominance in auditing the majority of listed companies. Limited competition has been cited as a potential source of conflicts of interest and lack of objectivity (The Economist, 2017).

Regulators have been actively pursuing the Big Four. Sir Jon Thompson, Chief Executive of the Financial Reporting Council, remarked to the *Financial Times*: "To be frank, one of the things that strikes you when you meet these people is they give people advice about how to run their businesses better, but sometimes they don't run their own business very well" (O'Dwyer, 2021).

Tolleson and Pai (2011) examined the impact of consolidation in the audit market. Companies seeking audit services face a "tight oligopoly," where the top four firms capture at least 60% of the market. Examples from the petroleum and air transportation industries show that the top two providers of audit services to these industries command more than 60% of the market, leading to interdependence. This implies that each Big Four firm must consider the reactions of their rivals when pricing products or offering new services (p. 58). In some industries, a single provider may dominate more than 60% of the market, leading to implicit collusion on pricing.

## Auditor Independence

When Thomas Cook collapsed, a question was raised about whether the independence of the group's auditor was compromised by the fact that it also offered permissible non-audit services (Kinder, 2020).

> *Even if accounting firms are banned from carrying out other services for audit clients ... they will still be beholden to the executives who hire and fire them. Just as important, the bond created by working closely together under pressure means that auditors too rarely challenge management (Mr. Hayward in The Economist, 2003).*

Previous research and practice have questioned the possibility of auditors maintaining an independent mentality when approaching their audit assignments. Bazerman et al. (1997) argue that audit failures do not primarily originate from deliberate behavior by an auditor but rather from the inability of auditors to psychologically separate themselves from their clients' interests. The structure of the audit–client relationship aligns two sets of interests. Management aims to portray their accounts in the best possible light, typically seeking a clean audit report from an auditor. On the other hand, auditors must perform their duties with true independence, objectivity, and transparency, adhering to professional standards, and avoiding any appearance of undue client influence on an audit opinion. However, auditors face conflicting pressures: maintaining a positive relationship with the client who hires and pays them, and the pressure to act professionally. This creates "the psychology of the impossibility of independence" (p. 91).

Psychological research on biases indicates that maintaining a mindset of objectivity and impartiality is challenging given the current institutional structures in auditing. Auditors struggle to maintain true independence because they receive payment from their clients and build long-term relationships with them. Additionally, unless banned by legislation, auditors might be involved in non-audit services. Advocates argue audit firms should be prohibited from providing non-audit services to their clients or establishing long-lasting relationships with them in order to maintain their independence (Bazerman & Moore, 2011, p. 310). Yet, this is not a simple or straightforward process. For instance, the EU already prohibits auditors from providing a list of non-audit services, such as tax services, valuation, and payroll services, to clients classified as public interest entities (PIEs) (EUR-Lex, 2014). Similar prohibitions exist in the USA. However, this has not eliminated the occurrence of hundreds of violations related to independence in any given year (Foley, 2024b).

While regulations and standards rightfully aim to reduce audit deficiencies related to intentional bias, much of the bias that might be at play is unintentional. Research on human judgment indicates that auditors often process information and evidence in a way that aligns with their own interests. This means problems can arise from unintentional biases that honest auditors have, which influence their judgments, rather than from intentional biases aimed at deception. Psychological research has advanced the notion of moral seduction, suggesting that judgment bias is often subconscious and not deliberate (Guiral et al., 2015). According to this research, "intentional corruption is probably the exception … unconscious bias is far more pervasive" (Moore et al., 2006, p. 16).

Many studies have addressed the issue of bias impacting auditor judgments and decision-making processes. For example, a study by Cassell et al. (2022) found that auditors' assessments of risk in a given year are influenced by experiences related to risk assessments made in prior years. While past experiences can be useful, they can also lead to confirmation bias, where auditors seek evidence that validates previous findings, making them less sensitive to emerging risks.

Several studies have identified numerous other biases that impact audit judgment. Beyond confirmation bias, which is the tendency to seek evidence that confirms an existing belief (O'Reilly et al., 2017), there are other biases such as anchoring bias (relying too heavily on the first piece of information), groupthink (making decisions based on the consensus of others), availability bias (favoring information that is easily accessible), and selective perception (focusing on certain evidence while ignoring others due to personal biases) (Bazerman & Moore, 2011). The presence of self-serving bias in the auditing context has also been studied, and various studies indicate its presence. However, self-serving bias can be mitigated by factors such as group affiliations, suggesting that "accounting firms should continue to create and maintain strong group cohesion among audit teams and encourage auditors to affiliate with professional organizations" (King, 2002, p. 282).

For those who argue that auditors are susceptible to biases influencing their objectivity, the behavior of auditors provides evidence of their inability to be independent. For instance, as reported by Foley (2024b), Big Four accounting firms have admitted to hundreds of violations regarding auditor independence over the years. In 2022, PwC, for example, identified 129 breaches of independence rules impacting 74 clients. Similarly, Deloitte identified 129 breaches impacting 78 clients in 2022, and 107 impacting 53 clients in 2023. EY reported similar violations impacting 3% of audits in 2022.

Several studies have addressed this possibility of breach in auditor independence. Guiral et al. (2010) subjected 80 partners and audit managers to conflict-of-interest situations. They discovered that these situations could potentially lead to involuntary bias in their judgment, ultimately influencing their final decisions. The study did not uncover support for deliberate bias by the auditors. Other research suggests that sometimes auditors' judgments are biased due to their affect toward client personnel (Frank & Hoffman, 2015). Their study involving 119 audit managers uncovered issues related to "secondhand affective reactions," where auditors are influenced by information shared among audit personnel, leading to biased decisions based on interpersonal feelings rather than objective and impersonal audit evidence.

Several factors help mitigate bias and conflicts of interest (Anderson, 2000). First, auditors operate in a context of legal liability, where sizable penalties for audit failures discourage self-interest from overriding professional obligations. Second, audit committees play a significant role in balancing potential self-interest due to their leverage. Third, audit firms typically implement quality control systems, such as having another partner review audit work, which improves audit quality. Some studies have indicated that auditor expertise and education can mitigate biases resulting from various conflicts of interest (Guiral et al., 2015). However, despite those mitigative and corrective measures, psychological tendencies and biases still present challenges to auditors in consistently making objective audit judgments.

## CONCLUSION

This chapter addressed the audit profession and its evolution from ancient Egypt to contemporary times. While auditing has existed in various forms since ancient times, it was only in the last century and a half that it became a profession with established standards and professional bodies. Despite the evolution of this field, many challenges remain. These include variances in expectations regarding the role of the auditor, particularly in relation to fraud prevention, detection, and reporting. Additionally, the profession faces significant challenges related to attracting and retaining talent, the growing oligarchic nature within it, the dominance of a few large firms with increasing power and influence, and questions regarding auditor independence and biases in decision-making, whether intentional or not.

The following chapters will delve into these challenges, exploring the expectations gap, its drivers, outcomes, and potential remedies in detail. We will explore the commercialization of the auditing industry and the institutional logics that govern the profession. We will reflect on the role of institutional entrepreneurs who contribute to the advancement of the profession. We will explore the evolving role of the auditor and the identity transformations that have historically impacted the profession and its professionals. We will conclude with recommendations aimed at enhancing transparency and the role of the auditing profession in society.

# 2

# WHAT STAKEHOLDERS WANT: UNDERSTANDING THE AUDIT EXPECTATIONS GAP

*I don't want an auditor who is dynamic and creative. I want somebody I can trust*

A Senior Risk Manager (ICAEW, 2021)

In a Reddit discussion, a young auditor shared his experience as a new staff member at a Big 4 firm: "Auditing seems like a low-value, low-reward attempt to convince prospective clients that it is delivering something vital to their businesses, but from the inside, it looks like a scam. Should audits be worth more, and should clients be paying more for the time it takes to deliver an audit?" In response, one comment highlighted the various pressures on audit partners: "Partners work to ensure that the audit quality is good enough to sell and efficient enough to be profitable" (Reddit, n.d.). In contrast, an opinion piece in the *Financial Times* by a former head of global assurance at a Big Four firm noted that auditors fall short in providing useful information to stakeholders: "For decades, the auditing profession has been drifting away from stakeholders' interests and focusing on its own. Shifting from assurance to insurance would restore trust and introduce as much order as possible into the chaos of growing financial uncertainty" (Mouillon, 2018).

These perspectives encapsulate the dilemma faced by the auditing profession: providing audit assurance services effectively and efficiently while adequately signaling the real value that auditing offers. In theory, auditing provides external and independent reasonable assurance about financial statements, enhancing credibility and trust in a company's financial position. Decision-makers, whether investors, lenders, regulators, or other stakeholders, base part of their judgments on the audit report and assurance. However, the perceived value often falls short of expectations. Even when auditors perform their duties effectively and there are no indications of corporate or audit failures, there is a perception that auditing firms receive excessive compensation for their services.

Leaving aside additional services auditors may perform, such as non-audit services, the primary product they deliver is an audit report. This report, typically a few pages long, often represents months of hard work, data collection, document tracking, verification, analysis, and professional judgment involving tens or even hundreds of professionals at various levels within the audit firm. During a busy season, it would not be an exception for an auditor to work 75–80 hours a week, finding it very hard to establish work-life balance: "there truly are times when the demands of work make it feel impossible to spend time with the people I care about" (Siew, 2018). Stakeholders often lack a clear understanding of this substantial level of effort, leading to a perception gap regarding the value of the services provided. While this gap might be well understood in intangible services, it may be more pronounced in auditing.

The nature of auditing – being a service rather than a product – has significant implications for perceived value. Auditing shares many features that differentiate products from services. It is an intangible service; the audit report, as the outcome of the economic transaction between the company and its auditor, does not resemble a tangible product that a buyer can observe, experience, and evaluate (Groth & Dye, 1999). The purchased service is neither returnable nor exchangeable. The features of the service are not testable to the same extent as product features (size, volume, physical convenience, materials). The quality must be inferred, which is why the audit service provider's name – the Big 4 versus a smaller, less reputable firm – matters significantly. Others' evaluations of the service strongly influence this inference, rather than the clearer, more objectively identifiable criteria of the product. While positive testimonials from people make a difference in a product context, such referrals carry more weight in service encounters.

In sum, the complexity of auditing services makes assessing audit quality subject to numerous factors, including perceptions of users of financial statements and other stakeholders. These perceptions are largely subjective, reflecting inferences rather than clearly identifiable factual data. Most users – except some regulators and former auditors – are often less qualified than auditors in understanding the audit function. This increases the susceptibility of such users, including the media, to external influences, prompting them to sometimes draw imprecise or erroneous conclusions. These conclusions feed a cycle of lower perceptions of audit quality and higher expectations of what auditors need to do. This only intensifies the expectations gap, a long-lasting phenomenon that has proven resistant to change.

## THE EXPECTATIONS GAP

Scholars and practitioners in accounting have extensively discussed the expectations gap phenomenon. The expectations gap refers to the mismatch between what the public perceives auditors promise and what auditors understand they deliver. Some scholars describe this as a dichotomy between perceived promises and actual delivery (Haniffa & Hudaib, 2007; Lee, 1994). Others note it as a gap between beliefs about the auditor's role and audit objectives (Baker, 1993; Hassink et al., 2009).

Various terms have been used to describe this gap, including "familiar dichotomies" (Lee, 1994), differences in "judgments" (Kinney & Nelson, 1996), "beliefs" (Monroe & Woodliff, 1993), "sentiments" (García Benau & Humphrey, 1992), perceptions (Schelluch & Gay, 2006), or "views" (Bedard et al., 2012). An early definition by Liggio (1974) described it as "the difference between the levels of expected performance as envisioned by the independent accountant and by the user of financial statements." The ACCA defined it as "the difference between what the general public thinks auditors do and what the general public would like auditors to do" (ACCA, 2019, p.7). Based on these understandings, we offer the following conceptualization of the expectations gap:

> *Variances in perceptions between what auditors perceive their roles, scope of work, and levels of accountability/ liability to be, versus what the public perceives those to be.*

This gap reflects discrepancies in perceptions regarding the roles of auditors. The public often doesn't understand the profession enough to tell what an auditor can and should do. Stakeholders' demands often exceed what auditors consider necessary based on their understanding of auditing standards. This leads to further discrepancies related to accountability and auditor liability, as disputes arise over the extent of blame auditors should assume in cases of fraud, errors, and business failures. Given that there has been formal discussion on this gap at least since the 1970s, its persistence is astonishing. It appears that this gap is not narrowing, which some see as a sign of professional failure.

Drawing from decades of scholarly research on the subject, the ACCA breaks down the expectations gap into three distinct categories. First, the knowledge gap refers to the discrepancy between what the public thinks auditors do and what auditors actually do. This reflects a lack of understanding regarding the profession, professional responsibilities, and the standards and regulations guiding audit behavior. Many users of financial statements who rely on the audit report do not have enough understanding about what auditors actually do. These users may include investors or potential investors who operate in a completely different field. Media representatives advocating for increased auditor accountability may lack formal training in accounting or auditing. In certain countries, even members of the judicial system investigating corporate or audit failures may lack a solid understanding of what an auditor actually performs. If one views the knowledge gap as the primary contributor to the expectations gap, then remedies would focus on educating the public or users of financial statements. However, we cannot solely attribute the gap to a discrepancy in knowledge.

The performance gap constitutes the second component of the expectations gap. This refers to the difference between what auditors should do and what they actually do given a fair understanding of standards and regulations. The ACCA report provides an explanation of the performance gap:

> *This could be because of insufficient focus on audit quality; the complexity of certain auditing standards; or differences in interpretation of auditing standard or regulatory requirements between practitioners and regulators (ACCA, 2019, p.10).*

The notion of "insufficient focus on audit quality" essentially means auditors are not performing their duties properly. Critics who assert a significant relationship between the expectations gap and the performance gap primarily attribute the expectations gap to auditors' actions. Another explanation attributes the gap to ambiguous standards or regulations that lack clarity. This distinction between the role of the auditor and the role of the standard setters subdivides the performance gap into two categories: deficient performance and deficient standards (Hassink et al., 2009; Porter, 1993).

In some contexts, auditors are subject to multiple regulatory influences. Their responsibilities are determined not only by a set of standards but also by various laws that expand the understanding of what an auditor is supposed to do. For instance, codes of commerce in certain countries impose specific duties on auditors, potentially making them liable for a company's debts in the event of bankruptcy and asset deficit. This allows the court, based on a request from the bankruptcy trustee, the public prosecution, or on its own initiative, to charge the company's debts to members of the board of directors, the general manager, or any other person entrusted with managing or monitoring the company's business, including its auditors. In practice, the default has been to hold the auditor liable, and the auditor must demonstrate that they have approached their work appropriately and exercised due professional care (Daher, 2020).

The evolution gap refers to specific areas of audit where the public desires auditors to perform tasks not required by standards and regulations. This reflects the public's aspiration for a higher level of assurance, or even insurance, regarding the auditor's roles and responsibilities. For example, the general public might expect auditors to detect early signs of business failure and may even blame them for unforeseen business discontinuities. While the profession has standards regarding the auditor's responsibility for the "going concern" nature of businesses, the public often has a broader understanding of this responsibility. Auditors worry "that they are being seen as providing insurance against corporate failure" (The Economist, 2018b). They assert that their role does not replace the role of astute management, which implements effective business models to guarantee reasonable returns to shareholders (The Economist, 2018b).

Even when the public recognizes that auditors cannot provide insurance about the financial statements, calls remain for their role to evolve. For example, financial economist Joshua Ronen argues for an alternative model for auditing, one where auditors would cease to operate as providers of assurance about financial statements but instead offer "financial statements insurance." This model aims to align the incentives of auditors with those of investors, rather than having auditors succumb to pressures from companies' management (Ronen, 2010). This intriguing proposition, if implemented, would significantly change the profession itself and the positioning and identities of auditors. It might even lead to the creation of another competing industry that can offer a higher level of services to clients. Irrespective of the practicality of this proposition, it suggests an evolution in stakeholders' demands from auditors.

One of the most obvious, and perhaps most critical, gaps between auditors and other stakeholders pertains to the auditor's role in fraud (see previous chapter). Various stakeholders persistently lack clarity about the auditor's role in identifying fraudulent activity. Numerous studies have demonstrated an increase in stakeholder expectations of auditors with respect to fraud prevention and detection. In one study (Hassink et al., 2009), for example, business managers, bankers, and auditors were asked about their definitions of fraud and the auditor's responsibility for (1) detecting fraud, (2) investigating suspicions of fraud, (3) reporting on fraud in their audit report, and (4) resigning from their assignment when fraud is uncovered. Significant expectations gaps were found in 20 out of 35 areas. The study noted: "business managers, as much as bankers, have the unreasonable expectation that auditors are responsible for detecting non-material fraud or detecting fraud (both material and non-material) in the case of collusion" (p. 98). Despite the profession's progress in clearly defining the auditor's role in detecting fraud, the public sometimes fails to understand or accept this clarification. Some scholars note that the expectation of uncovering fraud remains a major driver of the expectations gap (Humphrey et al., 1993).

A gap also relates to the scope of what auditors should do, specifically which processes should be audited and to what extent. In terms of scope, there are two interrelated issues. The first issue relates to what auditors "can provide," given their access to expertise, resources, and technology. The second issue relates to what auditors "should provide," given the prevailing standards and legislation (Hammond & Sikka, 1996; Mayorga, 2013). This leads to the notion that while auditors could dedicate more resources and attention to achieving certain desired objectives (as understood by the public or an average investor), the prevailing rules and standards only require auditors to adhere to a certain set of objectives. In this case, an auditor "can" achieve a goal but may not be "required" to do so by professional standards. Being unaware of the profession's requirements, the public cannot tell what an auditor can and should do. They often have a broader understanding of what an auditor "should" do, which almost always exceeds what auditors, given their understanding of auditing standards, would expect.

Another level of discrepancy relates to matters of accountability and auditor liability. This involves disagreements over the level of liability that auditors should bear in cases of fraud, errors, and business failures. After almost every major corporate collapse, bankruptcy, or scandal, many stakeholders, including some investors and the media, question why the auditors were not able to uncover irregularities or fraud and call for holding them more accountable. For example, just two months before Lehman Brothers collapsed, the auditors expressed no reservations about certain transactions that, in retrospect, should have required closer attention (Richard, 2008). This led some observers to ask the oft-repeated question, "Where were the auditors?" (MacDonald, 2006; Thomas, 2018), and to hold auditors accountable for alleged negligence or wrongdoing. Major audit firms sometimes settle out of court, adding to the confusion about auditor liability. For example, consider the PwC settlement with MF Global (Fisher, 2017): "By settling before the jury had a chance to decide, PwC left open important questions about the extent to which an auditor can be held liable for its advice on complex accounting questions, which often resist a simple yes-or-no answer."

In sum, the public sometimes perceives financial statements to be the primary responsibility of the auditor, or a shared responsibility with the company's management. This is despite the explicit wording in the auditor's report, which states that financial statements are the responsibility of the company's management. While the profession has made strides in explaining the limits of the auditor's responsibilities, scope of work, and reasonable levels of accountability, this understanding is still not fully embraced by the public.

Auditors often refer to the wording of the audit report to show their roles and the limits of their responsibility. Many would still challenge auditors on this point, viewing the wording of the audit report as an attempt by the accounting profession to protect itself. This is why auditors are frequently legally challenged regarding their responsibility for corporate failures, fraud detection, or even corporate mismanagement, even when their reports clearly limit such expectations. Some assert that due to the increasing incidence of corporate failures, "auditors seem to have lost the battle against corporate convolution" as "ghosts of past frauds haunt the Big Four auditors" (Kells & Gow, 2018).

## DRIVERS OF THE EXPECTATIONS GAP

Prior research has identified several potential drivers for the expectations gap. These drivers can be attributed to the auditing profession itself, as well as to the public, users of financial statements, regulators, standard setters, the media, and others. Below, we elaborate on some of these.

### Self-regulation and Professional Evolution

Issues within the auditing profession itself contribute to the expectations gap. Some refer to the profession as a "self-interested profession" that regulates itself (Gay et al., 1998; Noghondari & Foong, 2009). The profession often protects its members by limiting their scope of work and reducing their liability in case of wrongdoing. According to some, the profession has failed to "adapt and evolve" (Cohen Commission, 1978), not keeping pace with contextual developments. The audit function is laden with tensions among various stakeholders: auditors, regulators, investors, and standard-setting bodies. As different parties push for their interpretations of what auditors should do, these tensions often lead to gaps. By seeking to protect itself, the profession may contribute to the expectations gap. Essex (2018) made the following observation in a letter to the *Financial Times*:

*The ability of senior company management to ensure their auditors are compliant has increased as the 'profession' has lost respect through this very compliance. A professional used to be defined as an expert who put principle before profit. Not so now apparently with auditors.*

Auditors themselves often feed the expectations gap through their various roles. For example, the growth of consultancy services offered by auditors, even under evolving regulations limiting such services, creates confusion about what auditors "should" and "can" do (Alexeyeva & Svanström, 2015; Citron, 2003). These role conflicts lead to misconceptions about audit roles and misinterpretations of audit outcomes (Mo Koo & Seog Sim, 1999). Auditors are also seen as deficient in effectively communicating with users of financial statements (Cohen & Knechel, 2013; Nørreklit et al., 2010) and often fail to properly educate users (Chandler & Edwards, 1996), leading to ambiguities and misinterpretations.

Moreover, the wide differences in public perceptions of audit quality provided by different firms (e.g., Big 4 vs non-Big 4) only feed these confusions. Intense competition (Okike, 2004), augmented by increased exposure through advertisements and media coverage, may create false perceptions about what firms can deliver. This relates to the problems of improper communication. Through interactions with key stakeholders, auditors may inadvertently create the perception that an audit is all about uncovering fraud and reporting it (Hammond & Sikka, 1996).

### Performance Deficiencies

In 2024, Chinese regulators imposed a six-month suspension on PwC China and fined them around $62 million for allegedly hiding fraudulent activities in audit failures associated with the property firm Evergrande (Leng et al., 2024). This is just one example of many other instances of regulatory bodies severely disciplining reputable audit firms for audit failures. Arthur Andersen stands out as the most striking example, having faced accusations of audit failures related to Enron. At the time, Arthur Andersen LLP was one of the largest public accounting firms, employing over 85,000 individuals in 84 countries. The US Supreme Court later reversed the initial conviction of obstruction of justice against the company for destroying records pertinent to the Enron audit. However, it was too late for the firm to recoup its market share, reducing the Big Five accounting firms to the Big Four.

Sometimes auditors underperform (Humphrey et al., 1993), and publicizing such performance deficiencies (Porter, 1993) may lead to litigation. This increases exposure to what auditors "did not do," putting more pressure on the profession and reinforcing public expectations. For example, in a publicized case about audits of Medicis Pharmaceutical Corporation, James R. Doty, PCAOB Chairperson, noted that the "company's outside auditor for more than 20 years – failed to fulfill their bedrock responsibility… The auditor's job is to exercise professional skepticism in evaluating a public company's accounting and in conducting its audit to ensure that investors receive reliable information, which did not happen in this case" (PCAOB, 2012). Such sentiments add to the perception that auditors' deficient performance contributes further to the expectations gap.

Some stakeholders have blamed the auditing profession for low-quality audits. In the UK, the regulatory body overseeing the auditing profession has lamented the "below-average" quality of audit work in banking (Jenkins, 2013). Audit failures have not contributed to a positive image, leading some to question whether auditing firms are indeed serving the public interest. Recent investigations by the International Forum of Independent Audit Regulators revealed quality issues in two-fifths of the audits reviewed. All four firms in the Big Four have faced substantial questions regarding audit quality and failures, including in some cases, alleged alterations in audit documentation (Harris, 2018).

Conflicts of interest are inevitable given the current auditing framework and their relationship with clients. Clients hire audit companies and pay their fees. In many cases, clients decide whether to reappoint the same auditors or switch to a different firm. According to Porter's analysis of competitive forces (Porter, 2008), clients can wield immense power, especially when they are large and significantly contribute to the revenues of audit firms. This dynamic can make auditors less willing to challenge or "stand up to their clients" (Mouillon, 2018). This led Ronen (2010) to assert that "auditors are supposed to be watchdogs, but in the last decade or so, they sometimes looked like lapdogs – more interested in serving the companies they audited than in assuring a flow of accurate information to investors" (p. 189).

## Standards and Regulatory Frameworks

Several studies have identified problems in professional standards that lead to gaps in expectations (Haniffa & Hudaib, 2007; Porter, 1993). Standards are sometimes unclear about certain elements of the audit process. Additionally, practice codes can be complex and difficult for non-professionals to understand (Llewellyn & Milne, 2007). Users' definitions and understandings of labels often differ from those of auditors (Lee, 1994), leading to different interpretations of what a specific standard means for audit practice.

The audit engagement is an opportunity for both parties to clarify their expectations and roles. However, uncertainties about the nature of the engagement can arise due to the complexity of the wording (Green & Li, 2012). Unclear or complex standards can expose auditors to higher levels of expectation from the end users of the audit report. Some studies also refer to the "inefficacy of the regulatory framework of accounting" (Cadiz Dyball & Valcarcel, 1999). In some countries, auditors face multiple expectations from professional standards and various regulatory codes, such as codes of commerce and banking codes. This multiplicity of regulatory structures can lead to rising expectations or confusion about the auditor's primary role.

## Public Perceptions and the Expectations Gap

Recent statements about the role and responsibility of auditors from investors, the media, the judiciary, and sometimes even regulators reflect a level of public obliviousness about the profession. Hassink et al. (2009) and Noghondari and Foong (2009) specifically highlight this ignorance among investors. There are low levels of knowledge about the audit profession, and society does not accurately understand the role of auditors (Mo Koo & Seog Sim, 1999). This inability to comprehend the real role of auditors naturally leads to rising expectations.

Users are generally uneducated about audit information (Christensen et al., 2012), which likely leads them to overvalue certain types of information not shared by auditors (Deegan, 2002). Users also do not understand the audit process, leading them to ask auditors to perform tasks that are unreasonable, creating a "reasonableness gap" (Porter, 1993). An audit expectations gap may still exist even if auditors perform professionally under acceptable standards. The public might still expect auditors to perform tasks that the profession finds unreasonable, such as uncovering every act of fraud. Additionally, they do not properly appreciate the risks and benefits associated with the auditing process, failing to comprehend the inherent limitations of audit work and outcomes (Reffett et al., 2012). Media attention following major corporate failures (Mayston, 1993) also contributes to the widening of expectations. This variance in knowledge can lead to misinterpretations by users of financial statements (Chen et al., 2012).

Many users encounter a significant information asymmetry concerning financial statements and the auditor's role (Hassink et al., 2009). Many users of financial statements, such as potential investors, benefit from auditing services without directly paying for them: "This lack of cost–benefit considerations may cause users to expect the greatest possible effort from auditors" (Hassink et al., 2009). Moreover, users often lack knowledge about the inherent uncertainty in financial statements (Christensen et al., 2012), which heightens their expectations. This knowledge gap is not limited to inexperienced investors; even bank loan managers may lack knowledge about what auditors do, which could potentially negatively impact their lending decisions (Noghondari & Foong, 2009).

## OUTCOMES OF THE EXPECTATIONS GAP

The auditing expectations gap has numerous purported outcomes, most of which are not positive for the profession. As this gap widens, conflicts among various parties with opposing interests increase, as people try to make sense of corporate failures, reputational risks, and questions about the meaning of the audit itself. We explore some of these outcomes below.

### Increased Litigation Risk

In 2004, the Italian food company Parmalat sued its auditors Grant Thornton and Deloitte for USD 10 billion, alleging that Grant Thornton auditors acted as "active conspirators" with the former management team. Deloitte faced accusations of repeatedly failing to report evident frauds. A US district judge dismissed the case 10 years later, citing a legal doctrine that prevents a company from recovering for its own fraud (Warmoll, 2013). Years earlier, the auditors settled a class action suit brought by investors out of court. This case underscores the intense scrutiny auditors encounter when a company falters.

Other cases similarly reflect attempts to shift blame to auditors for management's actions. For instance, in a case against KPMG, the Bank of Portugal was noted to be shifting responsibility to auditors for failing to identify issues at Banco Espírito Santo (Donn, 2018). Such high-profile cases underscore the increased litigation risk auditors face due to varying public expectations.

Studies have shown that auditors are highly concerned about the risk of litigation (Kinney & Nelson, 1996), which influences how they approach and perform their audits. Any increase in the scope of an auditor's work or liability can lead to higher audit fees, reflecting the heightened risk and responsibility auditors must manage.

### Conflicts at Various Levels

The expectations gap leads to conflicts among various stakeholders, most notably auditor–client and auditor–regulator conflicts. Conflicts between auditors and clients often involve demands for auditors to expand their scope of work and assume more responsibility for financial statements and corporate failures. Disagreements may arise over the conduct of audits, the expected scope of work, and issues of accountability and liability in cases of corporate failure (Awadallah, 2018).

Auditors also face role conflicts as they try to cater to the needs of various stakeholders simultaneously (Abiola, 2015; Mo Koo & Seog Sim, 1999). They must uphold professional standards and regulatory requirements while maintaining client relationships. This becomes more complex when auditors take on additional consulting engagements with audit clients, where regulations allow (Alvin Alleyne et al., 2006). These factors lead auditors to reconsider their audit approaches, often resulting in increased audit fees (Chen et al., 2012). However, higher audit fees can further feed the expectations gap, as companies paying more expect more from the audit.

## Lobbying and Overregulation

To protect their understanding of the profession, auditors often engage in aggressive lobbying activities. For example, PwC and EY have consistently ranked among the top 20 lobbying firms in the USA (Burnett et al., 2018). Auditors lobby to influence accounting standards, independence rules, and disclosure requirements. They also engage in activities related to implementing laws, such as audit rotation. As auditors try to manage expectations, they may push for laws that clarify their roles in ways that reflect their understanding of the profession. This can lead to overregulation, challenging the self-regulatory nature of the auditing profession (Baker, 1993). Accountancy and auditing boards may implement additional reforms to narrow the expectations gap in terms of performance and standards (Hassink et al., 2009).

Globally, there has been an increase in regulation. Regulation in the audit industry in the USA increased after the Great Depression with the Securities Exchange Act of 1934 and the establishment of the SEC, which mandated audits for listed companies. The profession remained mostly self-regulated through the AICPA until the Enron scandal led to the establishment of the PCAOB in 2002. In the UK, Holm and Zaman (2012) argue that a "crisis in confidence" has triggered a move away from self-regulation. Francis (2024) notes that regulation addresses market failures such as information asymmetry, lack of competition, and externalities. However, determining the optimal level of regulation is challenging, and overregulation remains a risk.

### Impact on Reputation and Credibility

The persistence of the expectations gap adversely affects auditor reputation, stakeholder confidence, and perceived credibility. Clients may switch auditors, which in turn impacts both the auditors' and the profession's credibility. High-profile audit failures or allegations of negligence significantly damage the industry's reputation. For instance, in 2023, Erica Williams, the PCAOB Chair, remarked, "We are seeing audit quality for both domestic and international firms trend in the wrong direction for the second year in a row" (Williams, 2023). Statements like this, often reiterated by regulators and users of financial statements, gradually erode the profession's trust.

Media bias against auditors serves not only as a driver but also as an outcome of the expectations gap (Cohen et al., 2017). Media coverage amplifies public frustration with corporate failures, creating a vicious cycle. Stakeholders increasingly question why auditors failed to detect fraud or corporate failures that were seemingly unexpected. As frustration grows, the expectations gap widens, harming auditors' reputation and heightening their exposure to litigation (Cohen et al., 2017; Cornell et al., 2012; Zhang, 2007).

### CONCLUSION

Lee et al. (2020) identify two key paradoxes related to false expectations in accounting scandals. The first paradox revolves around viewing the auditing function as a governance instrument. The public perceives auditors as mechanisms that report on corporate health, which often leads to surprise when corporate failures follow clean audit reports. The second paradox focuses on auditing as a fraud detection mechanism. This paradox emerges because "public accountants have consistently placed the major responsibility for detecting and preventing material accounting misstatements on senior managers – the very individuals whose honesty they are expected to rely on" (p. 425).

The persistence of the expectations gap, while bewildering to some, is not surprising. Conflicting interests, a self-regulating profession, increased media interest and coverage, and higher levels of regulatory interference are likely to exacerbate this gap unless these various stakeholders achieve a mutual understanding of the true role of auditing. Is this possible? This question will be explored further in the chapters to come.

# 3

# AUDITING: FROM PROFESSIONALIZATION TO COMMERCIALIZATION

*Do auditors have the moral education to ask community-based questions about corporate profits and the need for limits?*

*(Lehman, 2014)*

In a recent discussion with a senior partner from one of the big accounting firms, the partner mentioned that their market share in a particular region had grown exponentially, surpassing not only their direct competitors but also the growth rates of other regions within the same firm. The conversation focused heavily on size, growth, market share, and market leadership. There was no mention of the quality aspects of their services or what the public was gaining from their firm that others were not. Absent from the discussion was any reference to the core service where all audit firms began: the provision of assurance services by a professional and independent auditor. Instead, much of the conversation centered around lucrative multi-million-dollar governmental advisory projects unrelated to assurance and auditing.

Such a discussion would not have occurred 50 years ago. Arthur Wyatt, a renowned accounting scholar and practitioner, highlighted the decline in accounting professionalism in his 2003 speech to the

American Accounting Association titled "Accounting Professionalism – They Just Don't Get It!" noting that: "Too often the accounting firms... have not met the standards of professionalism that the public can rightfully expect from the leading accounting firms" (Wyatt, 2004). The transition from a professional mindset into a commercialized one has been highly controversial. Some view this as a regrettable shift, while others see it as a natural evolution reflecting the industry's growth and the changing conditions in which it operates.

The accounting profession was not always about size, market share, market leadership, and growth. Accounting firms often started as small, value-driven entities emphasizing a professional ethos. Over time, many firms have grown enormous, driven by profits and a keen desire for growth and market influence. These firms began extending their services beyond conventional auditing and tax work in the 1960s, a trend that continued through the 1980s and 1990s (Greenwood et al., 2002). The introduction of computer technology and the financial opportunities it offered facilitated this transition. As consulting services expanded, they became a substantial source of income for these firms, often surpassing revenues from auditing and assurance services. This shift led to a decline in the profession at large, compromising the perceived integrity and independence of auditors and decreasing public trust.

A visit to the websites of the big accounting firms reveals the evolution of the profession and how its biggest players see themselves and what they offer. The websites are strikingly similar, hinting at a convergence of industry culture and a shared understanding of their current standing. Terms such as "clients," "measurable results," "transforming organizations," "boosting shareholder value," "help clients realize their ambitions," "cost reductions," "success," "positive difference in society," and "tackling big challenges" are commonly used.

One firm's introductory page, "What We Do," features the word "clients" five times, but mentions "audit and assurance" only once, amidst a range of other services such as consulting, financial advisory, risk advisory, and tax. The websites of other firms showcase a diverse range of vision and strategic offerings, with audit and assurance services being prominent but not the sole or most significant services.

The perception from scanning these websites is one of grandiosity – highlighting the number of offices, the six-figure number of employees, market size in billions of USD, legacy (year established), and extensive community and social responsibility efforts. Accounting firms have changed over the years; this change is evident in organizational cultures, which represent the soft fabric that guides people's behavior inside organizations.

## WHAT ORGANIZATIONAL CULTURES?

Organizational cultures reflect shared and often hidden beliefs, norms, and values that shape how individuals behave inside an organization and set the stage for expected and accepted practices. The Competing Values Framework (CVF) (Cameron & Quinn, 2005) is a popular approach for understanding and assessing organizational cultures. This framework is particularly useful for analyzing the shift in organizational cultures within the accounting industry, highlighting a transition from an ethos of professionalism to a culture of commercialization. The CVF categorizes firm across two dimensions, leading to four types of organizational culture. The two dimensions are (1) "flexibility and discretion" versus "stability and control" and (2) "internal focus and integration" versus "external focus and differentiation." These dimensions lead to four types of organizational culture (Table 3.1).

**Table 3.1. Four Types of Organizational Cultures.**

1. **The clan culture** prioritizes flexibility and internal focus. Firms that emphasize collaboration and team environments typically adopt this culture. Many small family businesses and emerging businesses adopt such a culture.
2. **The adhocracy culture** prioritizes flexibility and an external focus. This is typical of firms that emphasize innovation and experimentation, as well as a desire to seek opportunities. This is typical of firms in the technological industry, particularly those that value pioneering innovation.
3. **The market culture** prioritizes stability and an external focus. This is common among firms that prioritize maintaining a competitive edge, focusing on market share, achieving goals, and maximizing profitability.
4. **The hierarchy culture** emphasizes stability and internal focus. Established firms, often larger in size, typically focus on implementing efficient processes and operations.

Accounting firms have traditionally started as small businesses, where clan culture was dominant. As they grew, it was natural for them to adopt a hierarchical culture, given the nature of their services and the industry's emphasis on professionalism and regulatory compliance. Over time, however, organizational cultures have shifted into emphasizing customer centricity, market orientation, competitive advantage, and profitability.

Thus, currently, it would not be amiss to conclude that aspects of market culture characterize the organizational cultures of large accounting firms. This culture prioritizes exploration over adherence, promotes market growth over stability, and values competitive advantage over procedures or compliance. With such a culture comes a focus on competition and growth, leading to increased demands on employees to meet expectations. Many accounting firms now place high demands on their employees, reflecting industry practices where excessive working hours are the norm. A study reported that it is common for employees to work between 10 and 14 hours a day, leave the office at midnight or even the next day, and be expected to work on weekends and public holidays (Ruiz Castro, 2012).

Different institutional pressures and external events influence the evolution of accounting in various countries and geographic contexts, but the convergence of the accounting profession to its current state appears to be global in nature. As Ruiz Castro (2012, p. 548) notes, "organizational cultures of international accounting firms and the professional identity of accountants are similar in different cultural contexts." One symbol of this convergence is the power and reach of the Big Four accounting firms, which have extensive operations worldwide. These firms have attained prestigious positions in society, leveraging their technical capabilities and core competencies, as well as their extensive marketing power and reach, to advance their brand and positioning. Many smaller firms try to emulate the practices of larger firms, hoping to join what they perceive to be an elite class of firms.

How did the accounting profession transition from an overwhelmingly professional mindset (a prevalent professional "logic") to a commercialized one? Thornton et al. (2005) trace the evolution of the accounting profession in the USA since the 19th century, which could provide an explanation. Multiple events, regulations, technological advances, corporate fiascos, and audit failures, along with business advancements, impacted the profession and influenced the transition from a purely professional institutional logic to a market-focused logic. Early institutional entrepreneurs left their mark on the profession, leading it to adopt values related to professionalism, independence, and transparency. Other parts of the world followed similar trajectories, borrowing UK and then US practices. In regions new to auditing, these entrepreneurs introduced the concept of an audit function to add legitimacy to a company's financial accounts. Self-regulation also marked this period, with implications for decades to come. The profession gained a reputation for giving credibility to financial statements, and associations of professional accountants emerged to guide professional behavior.

The financial crash of 1929 was a landmark event influencing the profession. Various regulations passed after the crash required the audit of certain entities, further solidifying the profession's societal standing and role in financial trust. Thornton et al. (2005) indicate that the post-World War II period witnessed the transition from fiduciary logic to corporate logic. Starting in the 1950s, companies requested more services from audit firms, and the profession was willing to transition into non-audit services. The AICPA in the USA endorsed this inclusion. This period saw a growing recognition of the significance of audit firms operating under a commercial logic, emphasizing competitive advantage, customer service, and profitability.

The 1970s and 1980s saw increased competitive pressures and growing recognition of the risks associated with pure commercial logic. Codes of conduct were altered to mitigate such risks, regulating advertising, competitive bidding, and commissions. The commercialization of the profession increased, and the Big Eight firms emerged, reflecting a growing recognition of the role of size, market share, and industry leadership. Several corporate failures occurred during this period and the subsequent decades, leading to a growing discourse about the role of non-audit services in compromising objectivity and independence. The Enron scandal and the ensuing Sarbanes-Oxley Act were landmark events that did not alter the industry's move toward increased commercialization.

Throughout this period, marketing terminology and concepts began to infiltrate the profession through interactions with marketing professionals. Accounting firms started to implement marketing tools and instruments within the boundaries of the codes of conduct. This inclusion only intensified competition among the large accounting firms, and the integration of firms into the Big Four further reinforced the commercial logic dominating the profession.

As it stands now, the profession is an immense industry with many major and smaller players. The Big Four accounting firms are large, extensive, powerful, and prestigious, and their actions often reflect positively, though sometimes negatively, on the entire industry. On one hand, society appreciates the role these companies play and the importance of having big, experienced firms serving various stakeholders' interests. On the other hand, the expectations gap persists, often leading to heavy criticism of the industry and its main players. The profession's highly admired power, reach, and impact often serve as grounds for condemning the industry and its large firms. Often criticized for its aggressive lobbying, increased commercialization, and relentless desire to protect itself, the accounting profession reflects a powerful market, commercial, or corporate logic. Increased calls for the profession to reform itself have resulted, with many arguing that the industry urgently needs structural transformation (Humphrey et al., 2021).

## PROFESSIONAL LOGICS VERSUS MARKET LOGICS

The perspective of institutional logics elucidates the behavior dynamics of institutions and their actors (Thornton et al., 2012). An institutional logic refers to the values and rules that people use to understand social reality, guiding their behaviors (Fathallah et al., 2020; Thornton & Ocasio, 1999). Entities and individuals within those entities are often subject to multiple institutional logics, which can sometimes be in harmony but at other times conflict. When faced with demands from conflicting institutional logics, organizations and individuals must employ various mechanisms to manage this complexity (Greenwood et al., 2011). Many studies have explored this phenomenon across multiple industries and settings. Various factors determine the precedence of one set of logics over another, making it challenging to understand how conflicting pressures impact people and their decisions.

## Professional Logics

A professional logics perspective in accounting entails that a professional accountant or auditor prioritizes professional behavior and adherence to ethical standards: "being a professional traditionally meant valuing expertise and knowledge, adhering to a set of professional norms, believing that public accounting is a calling, and prioritizing the protection of the public interest" (Daoust, 2020, p. 3). Early collective actions to establish associations of professional accountants reflected a desire to position accounting as a prestigious profession with its own rules, processes, and codes of conduct. The early founders of accounting associations typically held the greatest standing within the profession: "they saw accounting as part of a moral order and sought to separate themselves from 'less qualified' practitioners" (Richardson, 2017, p. 128).

Being part of a professional order serving the public interest entailed less attention to profit-seeking behaviors and less obsession with market leadership or dominance. For instance, various regulatory or professional agencies banned or heavily regulated advertising for accounting services. Accounting and auditing services were positioned as services for the collective good, and advertising was viewed as incompatible with this perception. This reflected an emphasis on integrity in communication and a desire to protect the profession's image and prestige. One of the first restrictions on advertising came from the American Association of Public Accountants (forerunner of the American Institute of Accountants) in 1894, which stipulated that "all members (of the AAPA) be prohibited from advertising their vocations, but insertion of a card in journals giving profession and address is permissible" (Wood & Sylvestre, 1985). This reflected the notion that "Accountants wanted to be a profession, and advertising was believed to be unethical... [and] lowered the dignity of the profession as a whole" (p. 59; 61). In 1948, the Code of Professional Ethics noted that "A member shall not directly or indirectly solicit clients by circulars or advertising, nor by personal communication or interview not warranted by existing personal relations" (AICPA, 1948). In 1973, the AICPA adopted a clear prohibition on advertising: "A member shall not seek to obtain clients by solicitation. Advertising is a form of solicitation and is prohibited" (AICPA, 1973). However, the profession had to take a sharp turn against this prohibition in the late 1970s. In the landmark case Bates v. State Bar of Arizona, involving two lawyers from Arizona who promoted their legal services through an advertisement, the Supreme Court ruled in favor of the lawyers, noting that advertisements represent a form of protected free speech. This ruling impacted the accounting industry, leading the AICPA to lift its ban on advertising in 1978/1979, rephrasing the ban as follows: "A member shall not seek to obtain clients in a manner that is false, misleading, or deceptive" (Millspaugh, 1995).

## Commercial Logics

The other institutional logic at play is commercial logic, which emphasizes market orientation and competitive positioning within the industry. Over time, the accounting industry has gradually adopted a commercial mindset (Willmott & Sikka, 1997), reflecting a growing emphasis on financial interests, competitive positioning, and market leadership (Chesser et al., 1994). Within this logic, customer centricity is paramount, and profitability and market growth are key performance indicators.

In a capitalistic society, there is nothing inherently wrong with firms seeking to serve clients efficiently and effectively for profit. Some researchers have noted the potential positive influences of commercialization, arguing that increased commercialization enhances firm identity, fostering a sense of belonging that subsequently elevates auditors' subjective well-being (Ponomareva et al., 2020). However, the application of commercial logics has faced significant scrutiny, prompting the profession to deeply reflect on its transformation over time. This gradual transformation has seen an increasing emphasis on the commercial skills of accountants, often at the expense of other valuable qualities like honesty, trustworthiness, and technical capability (Hanlon, 1994).

There is ample evidence that the auditing profession has become more commercialized. Firms compete for market leadership, use aggressive advertising, and uphold common corporate ideals of "business acumen" and "client welfare" (Dunne et al., 2021). The Big Four accounting firms often choose renowned financial centers for their office locations, reflecting a strong emphasis on commercial values (Cooper & Robson, 2006). Other companies with branch offices that want to create a similar image to the Big Four embrace comparable commercialization principles (Hanlon, 1994). This reflects a culture in which the "profit motive informs the dynamics of accounting firms" (Sikka et al., 2009, p. 138); their additional advisory services beyond audits further contribute to their capitalistic image (Sikka, 2008).

Many studies have empirically traced this phenomenon. For example, Picard et al. (2014) examined the extent to which the profession's cultural representations, as exemplified in promotional materials, have been consistent with the argument for increased commercialization in the accounting profession. They reviewed and analyzed brochures from the *Ordre des comptables agréés du Québec* (OCAQ) over four decades. They uncovered a change in "logic" or mindsets consistent with the commercialization thesis that evolved over the years, consolidating in the early 2000s. This represented a culmination of evolution in the profession, leading to "an erosion of professional values and a significant shift toward commercialistic values" (Gendron & Suddady, 2004; Picard et al., 2014, p. 94; Suddaby et al., 2009; Wyatt, 2004).

Firms have not only adopted this changing spirit in the profession, but they have also transmitted it to students and future professionals. While this transformation is not complete due to safeguards preserving some elements of professionalism, aspects of commercialization seem to prevail (Picard et al., 2014). The profession is not only aware of this dichotomy in discourse but is also "at peace" with the harmonious coexistence of both logics.

Several factors have driven commercialization, including marketization, intense competition, the growing power of accountancy firms, ineffective regulation, and a self-regulated industry. The introduction of marketing expertise into the accounting profession in the 1980s (Picard, 2016) led firms to prioritize growth through increased marketing efforts. Over the years, there have been multiple opportunities for accountants and marketers to interact at conferences and other encounters. These complex interactions facilitated the gradual change of mindset within the accounting profession and the adoption of marketing practices that were for about 80 years deemed unethical, illegal, and not reflective of a professional demeanor (Picard, 2016). The Big Four and larger accounting firms took the lead, but smaller firms followed suit (Table 3.2). This process has been referred to as a "gradual process of marketization" (Picard, 2016; Wedlin, 2008):

> *Marketization entails an increasing presence and acceptance of marketing ideology and implementation of marketing initiatives with the expressed aim of developing markets and increasing profits ... marketization does not mean a passive adaptation to marketing principles and techniques; it is an active process to construct marketing for professional services by interacting with marketing experts (Picard, 2016, p. 8).*

**Table 3.2. Marketing & Sponsorships by Accounting Firms.**

It would not be unprecedented to see the brand of a Big Four on a race car. While sponsorships and partnerships entail a level of professional engagement, community philanthropy, or corporate social responsibility, this begs the question of whether this is becoming of a professional services firm. A quick search for corporate sponsorships of the Big Four provides significant examples.
1. Deloitte: Worldwide Olympic Partner (Olympics, n.d.); various sports events;
2. PwC: sponsorships of cricket tournaments;
3. EY: sponsorships of the Women's Tennis Association;
4. KPMG: sponsorships of golf tournaments.

Second-tier accountancy firms have also joined such initiatives:
1. BDO: sponsorships of rugby events;
2. Grant Thornton: sponsorships of cricket events;
3. RSM International (n.d.): sponsorships of sports events and TV programs (Shark Tank).

In 2018, Deloitte launched a global advertising campaign targeting airports worldwide, emphasizing a unified brand message: "one global brand delivering one global voice." The campaign aimed to enhance brand perception, differentiate the firm from competitors, and engage employees globally. It highlighted Deloitte's expertise in technology and its ability to deliver business value in an era of rapid change, focusing on themes like cybersecurity, digital transformation, AI, innovation, smart cities, and the future of work.

The campaign and Deloitte's website messaging focus on creating connections and making an impact, with less emphasis on specific services like audit and assurance. Similar to Deloitte, other firms such as KPMG, PwC, and EY also present audit and assurance as components of a wider range of services, emphasizing areas like AI, technology, Environmental, Social, and Governance (ESG), risk management, marketing, strategy consulting, and business transformation. All of this suggests that big accounting firms and smaller aspiring firms have been utilizing professional marketing and communication campaigns to reflect the changing nature of the industry and its growing commercialization (Deloitte, n.d.; EY, n.d.).

---

Audit firms have adopted the foundational pillars of market orientation – customer focus, coordinated marketing, and a profitability focus (Kohli & Jaworski, 1990). While these principles are commendable in business, they could potentially raise questions – if not properly approached – in professional services like auditing, where serving a broader range of stakeholders is crucial. The risk of a shift from an overwhelming desire to serve the public into a market orientation includes the potential to decrease audit quality and increase audit failures (Citron, 2003; Humphrey & Moizer, 1990). Commercialization has been linked to unethical behavior and a degradation of auditor independence (Broberg et al., 2018). Performance pressures, such as meeting cost budgets and time targets, and perceived role conflicts increase the likelihood of dysfunctional behaviors in auditing (Pierce & Sweeney, 2004; Sori et al., 2010; Windsor & Warming-Rasmussen, 2009). The proliferation of non-audit services has further impacted the perception of auditor objectivity and independence (Sori et al., 2010).

The collapse of Enron highlighted the link between commercialism and its drastic impact on stakeholders, often associated with audit failures (Gendron & Spira, 2010). A study of former members of Arthur Andersen after its collapse noted that many linked a spirit of commercialism to audit failure: "through the collapse of Enron, the link between commercialism and audit failure gained significantly in reality in the eyes of a majority of our interviewees" (Gendron & Spira, 2010, p. 296). Many within the firm viewed the move toward more commercialization as "years of insanity." In summary, many believe that commercialization creates an organizational environment that undermines professionalism and independence, qualities that the audit profession has long championed.

## Legitimizing Commercialization

Accounting firms and professional auditors are aware of the increasing shift toward commercialization and market orientation. They also recognize the need to balance the conflicting demands on the profession, whether it involves respecting its legacy or advancing it into the new era to continuously attract new talent. In this process, commercialization is often legitimized through various mechanisms that aim to reconcile conflicting logics and perceived inconsistent institutional demands. Dermarkar and Hazgui (2022) identified several mechanisms by which professional accountants legitimize commercialization:

1. **Theoretical rationalization "Auditing is a business."** This mechanism legitimizes commercialization not based on a moral argument but rather on cognitive legitimacy – "how things are." Auditing is perceived as a business like any other that provides services to willing clients. The party utilizing the audit report is seen as a "client" rather than a "user" or beneficiary, making the client the primary stakeholder. The importance of other users is thus downplayed.

2. **Personal authorization: "A client is king" mindset.** This strategy relates to customer centricity, where the customer is invariably the company that hires the auditing firm and pays its fees. The "client as king" ethos dominates the interaction, significantly impacting the professionalism and independence of the auditor. The client becomes the dominant party, and

the auditor's role includes ensuring smooth interactions and justifying their fees. Here, terms such as "customer satisfaction" and "customer centricity," which are dominant terms in marketing literature, become frequently used. Given that the product that auditors provide is intangible (an audit opinion) with no tangible value that can be readily felt –at least in comparison to other types of services –, auditors find themselves often trying to justify their fees to the client and on a relentless journey to signal the value to the clients. This creates additional tension in the relationship between the auditors and their clients.

3. **"Instrumental rationalization: An imperative for the future of the audit profession."** The third mechanism for legitimation, as outlined by Dermarkar and Hazgui (2022), revolves around the notion that the auditing profession has been evolving, and transitioning into a commercial mindset is a crucial step in the right direction for the future of the profession. In this case, clients and auditors alike view "old auditing" as incapable of persuasively showcasing its worth. Just a reconfiguration of the value of auditing and its future growth would entail an evolved mindset where some commercialization is key to creating the right incentives. Also, auditors often refer to the additional services they can offer (e.g. consulting services) to provide additional legitimacy regarding the value they offer. Offering such additional services becomes a vehicle to persuade clients and persuade auditors themselves as to the value they are providing.

Auditors use various mechanisms to discredit any perceived clash between professional and commercial logics. Some argue that commercial considerations are unavoidable (Citron, 2003). Even some regulatory or professional statements, such as the UK accounting profession's 1996 Statement on Integrity, Objectivity, and Independence, may inadvertently promote commercialization (Citron, 2003):

> ....*the UK accounting profession's 1996 Statement Integrity, Objectivity and Independence which was*

*introduced at a time when the increasing commercialization of the profession was provoking heightened levels of criticism both of auditors and of the regulatory framework within which they were operating ... the new statement reflects and indeed helps promote this increased commercialization (Citron, 2003, p. 267).*

Commercialization in accounting can be understood within a capitalistic framework, where the purchase and sale of accounting labor are straightforward economic transactions (Siôn Owen, 2003). However, there are risks associated with the commercialization of certain professions. For instance, in the healthcare industry, hospitals procure medical expertise and subsequently sell healthcare services to patients, typically billing on the basis of professional fees and costs, with a margin included. This does not mean it is acceptable to approach medical care purely from a commercial perspective. The public service aspect of healthcare is evident, whereas in accountancy, it is less prominent. The profession may gradually shift its focus to purely economic transactions, neglecting to serve relevant stakeholders.

Loscher and Kaiser (2020) identify three mechanisms by which the auditing profession harmonizes these competing logics: ambivalence, assimilation, and integration. Auditors often try to combine professional and commercial goals through instruments like client acceptance processes and risk-management approaches. This leads firms to embrace a "double culture" where both values are adopted and prioritized. These arguments by the profession suggest that "management procedures in public accounting firms revolve around prioritizing the time use of public accountants in an efficient yet simultaneously quality-ensuring way." (Loschher & Kaiser, 2020, p. 85). Whether this assertion by auditors can be realistically implemented across cases is doubtful. Indeed, many instances allow for the assimilation or integration of values of professionalism and commercialism. It is those few instances that might be rare in occurrence but significant in importance and implication that prioritizing might pose dilemmas for the auditor. In those instances, auditors might be confused about which values prevail. Despite millions of high-quality audits conducted annually, the fewer audit failures still prove that sometimes commercial values prevail, tainting the profession and overshadowing successful audits.

In sum, while commercialization can enhance firm identity and customer satisfaction, it also risks degrading auditor professionalism and independence. Audit failures linked to commercial pressures highlight the potential negative impacts, overshadowing the many successful audits conducted annually.

## IDENTITY

Broberg et al. (2018) explored the factors driving commercialization, noting that both professional and organizational identities drive it in audit firms. "Forging a profession's identity involves developing a mutual understanding of values, beliefs and ways of thinking that is internally shared and externally recognized, providing the cultural underpinnings necessary for the new profession's legitimacy" (Gibassier et al., 2020, p. 1450). DeCoster and Rhode (1971) highlighted a disconnect between the prevalent image of an accountant and the "desired image" sought by the accounting profession. This reflects a consistent desire by the profession and the professionals to go beyond the prevalent images by the public. Indeed, there have been shifts in the portrayal of accountants in movies and media, with some depictions being positive and others not. Identity reconstruction has been necessary for several reasons, including:

1. **Attractiveness and Dynamism.** Professionals naturally desire to belong to an attractive and dynamic group rather than a dull and uninspiring one. This is not merely a cosmetic transformation or an attempt to manage self-esteem. There is a significant risk to the profession, especially in today's world, if outdated stereotypes continue to prevail. The future of the profession and its ability to attract young talent would face serious implications.

2. **Professional Transformation.** The profession itself has been undergoing significant transformations, and identity work or reconstruction is both normal and expected. The shift from

traditional professionalism to commercialization, whether welcomed or not, suggests a parallel transformation in professional identities. The image of a traditional professional auditor is different from that of a savvy, market-oriented, entrepreneurial auditor.

## The Accountant Identity

Daoust and Malsch (2019) noted that auditors, like other professionals, develop social identities related to the nature of their work and the type of firm they work in. In this regard, they encounter several tensions as they balance their inner selves with their organizational identities:

> *As a result, they are often torn between organizational commitment and professional loyalty between the requirement to develop business and the duty to protect the public interest ... In other words, they often struggle to obey a "commercial professional logic" and a "technical-professional logic" at the same time.*

The stereotype of an accountant often portrays them as diligent and conscientious, but this image does not always confer high social status (Leão & Gomes, 2022). Richardson et al. (2015) developed a conceptual framework to explain stereotypes of accountants:

- Scorekeeper: A positive yet traditional perspective that emphasizes diligence and trustworthiness. The scorekeeper demonstrates conscientiousness and meticulous attention to detail, prioritizing accurate record-keeping and ensuring compliance procedures are followed.

- Bean counter: A negative and traditional view of an accountant as neurotic and awkward. This image suggests someone who focuses on minor details and is stereotypically lacking in interpersonal skills and the ability to think beyond prescribed procedures.

- Accountant guardian: A positive and contemporary portrayal of an ethical and adaptable accountant. This evokes an image of a person deeply concerned about the integrity of financial disclosure, driven by a concern for the public interest.

- Accountant–entrepreneur: A contemporary image but carries a negative perception of cunning and deception. This evokes an image of a shrewd accountant, a risk-taker, and business-oriented individual who is eager to find creative solutions for clients, even if some of those solutions do not meet high ethical standards.

## Identity and Professionalism

The question arises whether the profession's attempt to advance the image of the accountant and attract a youthful generation has inadvertently socialized some entrants into valuing entrepreneurial and deceptive behaviors over professionalism and ethics. Thus, the image of an accountant-entrepreneur might best describe contemporary perspectives of how an accountant should be. The education of accountants and their socialization in the organizations they join as young accountants or junior auditors popularizes this image. This evokes an image of a street-smart accountant who recommends creative solutions to clients, aggressively markets tax avoidance schemes, and prioritizes profit over the public interest.

## Risks of Stereotype Shifts

Jeacle (2008) notes how the stereotype of the dull bean counter, despite its evident shortcomings, has been associated with some positive traits, such as being trustworthy and honest. However, the author highlights the negative consequences of this stereotype, as it can hinder organizational behavior and obstruct the recruitment of future talent. Moving aggressively to propagate a different image of an accountant does not come without risks;

*in overexposing the case these recruitment messages potentially risk shattering some of the sincerity which has gradually built up around the scaffolding of the new and improved stereotype. Or perhaps, more seriously, they endanger the essence of the accounting qualification: its professionalism, its credibility and its integrity (p. 1317).*

The traditional image of an accountant as a bean counter "challenges the legitimacy of the accounting profession" (Christensen & Rocher, 2020) and has implications for the ability of the profession to attract younger generations of talented professionals. Christensen and Rocher (2020) traced the image through a review of cartoons in European French-language comic books for the period between 1945 and 2016. They noted the appearance of the image in the 1950s and 1960s and its disappearance in the 1970s. The 1980s witnessed a return of the image, but this declined again in the 1990s and on. In general, the image appears to have endured over time, albeit with occasional periods of decline. This persistence has triggered attempts to move beyond that stereotype into a more dynamic and appealing identity.

Recent literature has introduced the image of the "colorful accountant" as opposed to the "boring bean counter" (Christensen & Rocher, 2020; Jeacle, 2008). Dunne et al. (2021) explain how Big Four auditors sometimes utilize various impression management techniques to come across either as "colorful accountants" or "boring bean counters," depending on the audience. This would account for the evolution of the image of auditors over time into a more vibrant and alluring role as "entrepreneurs." This reflects the growing dominance of a commercial logic when accountants reflect on who they are or what their role is. In a study involving Big Four partners and directors, Spence and Carter (2014) note that the "traditional professional rhetoric about serving the public interest and acting with integrity and in accordance with ethical principles was notable only by its absence in the talk of our interviewees" (p. 955). Adopting an exclusive "commercial/entrepreneur/colorful" identity as the norm will inevitably lead to an increase in audit failures, which will significantly impact public perceptions of accountants, the perceived value of the accounting profession, and its contribution to society.

## Identity Crises and Reconstruction

Accountants frequently experience identity crises and continually need to reconstruct their identities due to increasing tensions, competitive pressures, and regulatory changes (Tomo & Spanò, 2020). Identity reconstruction became necessary, as the profession for a time remained inert and unreceptive despite enormous changes. There was a feeling that the professional body failed to adequately advocate for its members, leading accountants to seek image repair. One might wonder whether adopting the accountant–entrepreneur identity was the right strategy after an identity crisis, regardless of the pressures they face.

## CONCLUSION

The evolution of the auditing industry reflects a transformation from traditional professionalism to a market-oriented approach. The identity reconstruction of accountants has accompanied this transition, transforming them from the traditional bean-counter image to a more modern and outgoing accounting entrepreneur. However, this transition is neither absolute nor unidirectional. Auditors still face tensions as they navigate their true, perceived, and desired selves.

The implications of such transformations are numerous. Today's auditors need to continuously balance professional and commercial identities. While they are not advised to revert to the original image portrayed in the media, complete commercialization of their identities carries multiple risks, including an increased propensity for losing independence, professionalism, and public trust. Another important aspect relates to the nature of the auditing industry itself, as it tries to stay abreast of cultural transformations. If the original "boring bean counter" stereotype persists, the profession must navigate multiple risks related to its ability to attract talent. The profession must carefully navigate this delicate line.

Auditors also need to understand the implications of increased commercialization on audit quality and audit failures. With a growing desire to expand their businesses, auditing firms must not lose sight of maintaining the quality of their services. In short, one cannot call for a total abandonment of the traditional image of an accountant nor a complete resistance to the modern one. Commercialization has brought many benefits to the profession and created more opportunities for audit firms. However, auditors must remain cognizant of the need to uphold the core values of the industry, including its professional aspects and ethical standards.

# 4

# INSTITUTIONAL INERTIA AND INSTITUTIONAL ENTREPRENEURSHIP IN AUDITING

> *We are all united by a common mission to protect investors around the world – because audit quality protects people, from people saving for their families' futures, to workers getting jobs because companies can raise money to fund growth through sound, liquid capital markets.*
>
> Erica Williams, PCAOB Chair, 2023

Institutions are systems that create meaning, stability, and order through rules, norms, and shared beliefs; they "produce meaning, stability, and order" (Scott, 2003, p. 879). Scholars who study institutions, their role, and their evolution investigate why and how institutions embrace certain practices, become responsive and adapt to internal and external changes, or become defensive, static, and resistant to change. While organizations often develop procedures to handle changing environments, many struggle to transform due to long-standing practices that encourage stability rather than change.

### Factors Contributing to Institutional Inertia

The auditing profession has been slow to evolve due to several factors, including vested interests, strict bureaucratic structures, and deeply embedded norms. This resistance to change, known as institutional inertia (Aksom, 2022; Gilbert, 2005; Hannan & Freeman, 1984; Rosenschöld et al., 2014), has significant consequences on institutions and their stakeholders. These include operational inefficiencies, stakeholder dissatisfaction, legal liabilities, and loss of competitive advantage. While the auditing profession has made some progress over time in certain areas, it has struggled to make meaningful or timely advances in response to environmental changes. This struggle, particularly in terms of meeting stakeholder expectations, has widened rather than narrowed the audit expectations gap.

Several internal and external factors contribute to this inertia (Aksom, 2022; Gilbert, 2005; Hannan & Freeman, 1984). Internally, costs, prior commitments to existing practices, reliance on past traditions, and internal power dynamics play a role. Externally, legal restrictions, previous investments, and the fear of losing legitimacy due to drastic changes are significant drivers. Studies have shown that cognitive, behavioral, economic, and political factors (Haag, 2014; Mikalef et al., 2021) all typically contribute to institutional inertia in organizations. These same factors are also at play in the auditing profession.

Auditors often face a conflict between maintaining client trust and exercising professional skepticism (Rennie et al., 2010; Stevens et al., 2019). The fear of losing clients can cloud their judgment (Farmer et al., 1987), leading to various types of biases and failures in judgment. However, bias is more likely to arise inadvertently than as a result of deliberate choice (Moore et al., 2010). Auditors often fail to recognize these biases, making them resistant to regulatory changes. Additionally, practicing auditors are often unaware of their tendency to morally compromise due to conflicts of interest (Moore et al., 2006). Mental models that provide stability to institutions also make them resistant to change (Rosenbaum, 2022), and failing to update these models can harm the profession.

### Behavioral Inertia and Path Dependence

Behavioral inertia, or the tendency to repeat past behaviors, encourages maintaining the status quo (Henderson et al., 2021).

It is often the case that past decisions limit current possibilities (this is called Path dependence), which makes it difficult for organizations to improve (Mitchelmore, 2016). Established institutions and processes often make switching to new methods inefficient, thus reinforcing this inertia. Historical practices and traditions in the auditing profession have shaped its evolution and responsiveness; this often complicates transformational change. Even if a new practice proves to be more efficient, factors like costly technical lock-ins and long-standing audit processes create dependencies that are difficult to break (Khalil, 2013). Traditional education methods ("new" auditors continue to learn "old" practices) and a long history of self-regulation, which reinforce old routines and traditions, compound this lack of adaptability (Gilbert, 2005).

### Resistance to Change and the Status Quo

The status quo often optimizes individual gains and lowers transaction costs, making the profession resistant to change (Rosenschöld et al., 2014). Only when the costs of inaction surpass the costs of substantial action can we overcome institutional inertia. The perceived low likelihood of auditor prosecution and conviction discourages real reform (Moore et al., 2010). Instead of making audit work more comprehensive, the profession often pushes for restricting audit work, reducing accountability, and lobbying against audit rotation or joint audits (O'Dwyer, 2022; Thomas, 2021). Accounting firms use a variety of mechanisms to ensure institutional maintenance rather than institutional transformation. In this context, the Big Four function as institutional custodians, upholding the status quo, rather than acting as institutional entrepreneurs (Dunne et al., 2021).

Major events or "jolts" disrupt routines (Meyer et al., 1990). New practices go through a legitimation process to justify a departure from old routines (Greenwood et al., 2002). This legitimation process (Suchman, 1995) entails new activities becoming more normalized from both a practical and moral perspective. However, some institutions have developed systems that protect stability by reinforcing old habits and resisting change, thus becoming less sensitive to major shocks. This has indeed been the case for the auditing profession. While the profession has transformed itself while moving from the "professional" to the "commercial," it did not transform itself in terms of redefining its role or becoming more responsive to the external demands and stakeholder expectations. The audit profession has failed to sufficiently deinstitutionalize outdated practices or legitimize essential ones, thereby hindering significant transformation in certain areas. External events like corporate failures and penalties on audit firms have not led to considerable change. Instead, the profession often resorts to a defensive reflex, justifying its current practices and denying any wrongdoing, resulting in a swift return to the status quo or business as usual.

### The Impact of Scandals and Self-regulation

After the Enron and Arthur Andersen scandals, the profession faced increased threats to the self-regulation nature that had characterized it for a long time. However, this shift did not weaken the profession. In many countries, associations and accounting syndicates have continued to influence laws and resist some planned reforms. As a "transnational epistemic community" (Ramirez, 2012), large accounting firms are prominent internationally (Pereira et al., 2023). The profession's trend toward independent supervision has increased audit concentration (Elshandidy et al., 2021), leading very large and powerful firms to maintain their dominance (Humphrey et al., 2009). This meant that, despite stakeholder pressure, unfavorable media attention, and reported audit and corporate failures, the profession continued its efforts to persuade regulators to compromise regulation in their favor (Humphrey et al., 2009).

### Lobbying and Regulatory Influence

The profession frequently participates in lobbying campaigns to limit the scope or timeliness of new laws, and it actively engages with regulators to protect the interests of the profession (Allam et al., 2017). Their lobbying efforts even limit the recommendations of regulatory bodies like the PCAOB (Eaglesham, 2022). Professional associations and syndicates are also involved in such efforts on behalf of their members. For instance, the AICPA is known for its strong lobbying efforts on behalf of its members, augmenting the image of the profession being a self-interested and a "self-regulating monopoly" (Noghondari & Foong, 2009) that struggles to adapt and evolve (Cohen Commission, 1978). All of this contributes to making the public oversight authorities unduly influenced by the profession: "public oversight authorities are not 'genuinely' independent from the profession in many Member States" (p. 22), (EC, 2011). Instead of adopting new methods, the profession tends to defend its current practices and deny any wrongdoing during crises, quickly returning to old practices. Large accounting firms remain active in the standard-setting process (Ruhnke & Schmitz, 2019) and often oppose reforms that might compromise their market position.

## Embracing a New Mindset in Auditing

Changing from old to new practices requires a major shift in mindset. The auditing profession has been responsive in adopting new technologies over time and streamlining audit processes, but the mindsets of auditors, more or less, have remained the same for decades. One example of this resistance to change is the response to proposed legislation requiring audit firm rotation. The AICPA opposed this idea in 1992, and many auditors and organizations still hold this view. The profession's influence has watered down the regulations, even in countries that mandate audit firm rotation (Horton et al., 2021). Another example from Sweden illustrates this point: "Swedish auditors do not seem to be particularly eager to incorporate a more forward-looking quality control into their auditing domain. A possible explanation is that they feel secure on their own territory" (Öhman et al., 2006, p. 105).

Auditors often tend to stick to familiar practices and routines they learned during their training. Shifting this mindset requires cultivating an audit culture that genuinely prioritizes the public good and consistently reflects this value in all its actions, practices, and engagements with various stakeholders (Howieson, 2013).

Achieving this transformation demands the collective efforts of pioneering, disruptive thinkers and groundbreaking leaders who strive to challenge the status quo and initiate changes within their institutions.

## THE ROLE OF INSTITUTIONAL ENTREPRENEURSHIP

Institutional entrepreneurs are individuals who can drive significant change within institutions (Greenwood et al., 2002). They achieve this through their ability to "leverage resources to create new institutions or to transform existing ones" (Maguire et al., 2004, p. 657). These entrepreneurs possess particular abilities and status that allow them to effect change (Elliot, 2016). Such individuals have a degree of legitimacy that is not accessible to all actors (Hardy & Macguire, 2008).

### The Role of Big Accounting Firms

In the field of auditing, big accounting firms are well-positioned to play the role of institutional entrepreneurs though they often seem unwilling. They have better access to talent, resources, technology, and audit knowledge, which augment their influence. They lead the profession in negotiating with regulators and are often successful in securing concessions that protect their interests (Harber et al., 2023a; Harber et al., 2023b). The public recognizes this power, and companies engage with them not only for their perceived competence but also to enhance their corporate legitimacy (Tantawy & Moussa, 2023). These firms have the resources to invest extensively in multiple services, which smaller enterprises cannot match (Marriage & Rutter-Pooley, 2017). This augments power disparities and strengthens their hold on their particular marketplaces (McKenna, 2020). They also significantly influence the development of accounting standards and procedures, often resulting in audits "based on weak, compromised, and inconsistent rules that make failure 'normal'" (Shah & Grimstone, 2019). Some regulators' impact is sometimes "dwarfed" by their power (Marriage & Martin, 2017).

The big accounting firms' much-maligned dominance is precisely why they are well-positioned to act as institutional entrepreneurs. Institutional entrepreneurs enjoy distinguished levels of power, rank, and social positions that legitimize their actions; these are attributes that characterize these firms. However, two prerequisites must be met (Battilana et al., 2009). First, these agents of radical change must be capable and willing to undertake pioneering transformations. Second, they must actively participate in implementing these adjustments. While the Big Four have the potential to act as institutional entrepreneurs, their motivation to do so is unclear. Despite their potential to pioneer transformations in the industry, evidence suggests that big accounting firms, particularly the Big Four, have been unwilling to break up competition and lessen their market hold, hesitant to limit their provision of additional services such as consultancy, slow to transmit learning to smaller businesses (O'Dwyer, 2023), and aggressive in defending the status quo (Shah & Grimstone, 2019).

In relation to the above, there are two significant aspects that need to be addressed. The first aspect pertains to their potential role, which is currently unrealized, in developing constructive organizational cultures that diverge from the dominant commercialized cultures. The second aspect pertains to the importance of leading a process of rebuilding the professional auditor's identity. These two aspects are discussed below.

## A Return to Professionalism

As explained in the previous chapter, there are competing logics between "commercialism" and "professionalism" in the auditing profession (Loscher & Kaiser, 2020). The first logic implies profit-mindedness and a primary commitment to clients, while the second logic implies a primary obligation to the public interest (Whittle et al., 2016). Audit firms did not always possess commercialized cultures. Over time, the profession has dramatically shifted toward more commercialization (Dermarkar & Hazgui, 2022); the literature has widely discussed this evolution in culture (see, e.g., Broberg et al., 2018).

Auditors reject the premise that professionalization and commercialization are in conflict instead claiming that they complement one another. They employ numerous legitimation tactics to explain their economic activities by linking them to their public service endeavors (Dermarkar & Hazgui, 2022). Auditors employ "logic equilibrium" to balance these conflicting logics, typically prioritizing the commercial logic (Dunne et al., 2021). Professionals at smaller firms also adopt this mindset, striving to adopt similar cultures that emphasize commercialization and values such as success, dominance, and market leadership. They use various legitimation strategies to demonstrate that the commercialization of the profession improves audit quality (Harber & Willows, 2022).

More than just striving to achieve a commercial end, the auditing profession has the potential to break out of its current mold and become a vehicle for attaining a much-needed social purpose: "it is important to recognize the dysfunctionality of promoting a particular (standardized) form of auditing that is not compatible with ruling modes of corporate governance and social responsibility norms" (Humphrey et al., 2021, p. 458).

## Identity Reconstruction

As a result of the transition from professional to commercial, the present dominant image of a professional accountant is one of profit-mindedness and commercialization. Although some professional auditors may not consider it beneficial or a priority to reconstruct the identity of the professional auditor, doing so is a needed act of institutional entrepreneurship. The professional auditor is often portrayed as "a powerful superhero, a resolute leader who is strongly motivated by the prospect of success and attractive compensation" (Picard et al., 2014, p. 106). Young accountants have been socialized to fit that image. This, however, was not always the case.

## Evolution of the Professional Accountant's Image

At one time, the professional accountant's image was akin to that of an educator, a clergyman, a lawyer, or a medical practitioner, stressing a professional obligation to numerous external stakeholders (Jones, 1995; Thornton et al., 2005). A reliable and trustworthy auditor had a good reputation, was faithful to one's fiduciary obligation, and adhered to objective and well-defined professional standards. The increasing commercialization of the profession led to a shift in this image. Following the second world war, a competent and trustworthy auditor became linked with a large, developing, and resourceful organization, demonstrating a shift from fiduciary logic to corporate logic (Thornton et al., 2005). The need for expansion and the search for other revenue streams outside of auditing maintained the profession's existing logic, thereby keeping it in its current state of stasis. Professionals in the audit profession and those aspiring to join have embraced this value, increasingly making it an implicit initiation activity (Cooper & Robson, 2006).

## The Role of Institutional Entrepreneurs

Institutional entrepreneurs in the audit industry, particularly those operating in large and powerful accounting firms, have a significant influence on developing and reproducing the identity of the professional accountant (Cooper & Robson, 2006). Big accounting firms heavily influence the professional identities of accountants, including those in training or internships. Through immersion in communities of practice (training or internships), people develop those identities (Hamilton, 2013). Accounting trainees are more inclined to identify with the training organization (e.g., a Big Four firm) than with the professional body (an accounting association or syndicate) (Hamilton, 2013). This is further evidence of the salient role of the big accounting firms. According to Suddaby et al. (2009), "accountants working in Big 4 firms hold different attitudes about professional institutions and ideology than accountants in other types of firms" (p. 424).

## Changing the Accounting Stereotype

The accounting profession is no stranger to identity formation and reconstruction. They have been striving for years to change the accounting stereotype from the "boring bookkeeper" or "bean counter" to the "colorful accountant" to attract more students into the field (Jeacle, 2008). In a similar spirit, institutional entrepreneurs, particularly those embedded within the large accounting firms such as the Big Four, may take the lead in pushing this via recruitment drives that highlight role models who prioritize their public professional purpose above commercial aims. This has implications for how these companies advertise, share content on their websites and social media channels, create recruitment literature, arrange training and internship programs, publicize their accomplishments, report on their actions, and reward staff. Given their legacy, power, and reach, the big and powerful accounting firms are well positioned to effect cultural change and identity reconstruction, yet there are not enough internal or external incentive mechanisms to drive them in that direction.

## REDEFINING AUDITING

Given all the above, there is a dire need for auditing to be redefined, or as this book's title suggests, reimagined. This requires ongoing, relevant discourse concerning auditors' roles (Malsch & O'Dwyer, 2021). This discourse must include multiple stakeholders to achieve greater convergence on the "meaning of audit." Breaking free from the existing state of inertia that characterizes the audit profession necessitates that the profession become more open to a reinterpretation of the audit's meaning and significance.

### Embracing Change in the Audit Profession

Some audit firms have already shown indications of embracing such a conversation. PwC, for example, observed the shifting environment of auditing and acknowledged the "changing role of an auditor" in its comments on the Securities and Exchange Commission's proposed modifications to the auditor independence criteria (PwC, 2000). Despite such eagerness to participate in constructive conversation, the profession is often effective in watering down reforms and delaying genuine change (Harber et al., 2023a).

Big accounting firms, as prospective institutional entrepreneurs, have ample opportunities to advance the profession and enhance assurance services, contrary to the commonly held belief that they are maintaining the status quo. There are indications that if the profession does not handle problems properly, the audit expectations gap will expand even further in the future (Tiberius & Hirth, 2019).

### Addressing Auditor Responsibilities in Fraud Detection

One area where the audit profession may make a difference is the contentious issue of auditor responsibilities in identifying fraud. While providing absolute assurance about fraud detection would still be considered unreasonable, "the detection of material fraud is, and must continue to be, a priority within an audit" (House of Commons, 2019), and auditors must recognize increased pressures from other stakeholders in that regard. With the growth of technology and auditor skills, expectations will grow regarding the increased likelihood and ability of auditors to uncover fraud. This may be attributed to higher stakeholder awareness of advancements in artificial intelligence (AI) systems (Omoteso, 2012) and data analytics (DA), which have the potential to create the greatest change in how audits are conducted (Capriotti, 2014). If the audit profession fails to effectively handle these new technologies, it could worsen the audit expectations gap, as individuals hiring audit services may anticipate complete assurance rather than the legally required reasonable level of assurance (Earley, 2015). Auditors need to be aware of the expanded, and perhaps growing, levels of assurance expected by stakeholders.

### The Shift Toward Real-time Auditing

With the advent of technology, several stakeholders' expectations in other areas have also shifted. The completion of audits sometimes occurs months after the fiscal year ends, which is a significant limitation of traditional auditing (Carlozo, 2017). Waiting for a long period of time before an opinion on historical data is issued is becoming more unacceptable to companies and users of financial statements. These stakeholders want auditors to provide assurance much closer to the transaction time. New technologies and tools in AI and big DA are enabling stakeholders to increasingly demand "continuous real-time auditing" (Betti et al., 2024; Michael & Dixon, 2019; Salijeni et al., 2021).

Thus, reimagining auditing and the function of the auditor entails shifting from assurance of historical data to assurance of real-time data (Tiberius & Hirth, 2019). Additionally, auditors are increasingly being asked to explore modifying the definition of an audit to provide assurance on future activities, rather than solely giving assurance on past actions (Hossain & Mitra, 2022). While this may be too much to ask and would change the nature of the profession itself, it indicates shifting stakeholder expectations. Auditors need to embrace technology not just to improve audit efficiency but also to understand its consequences for audit accountability and stakeholder expectations.

## Expanding Assurance Services Beyond Financial Information

Another area in need of reimagination is the assurance of non-financial information. Stakeholders and legislative bodies are contemplating shifting from primarily financial information assurance to assurance of non-financial information as well. Providing a wider range of assurance services (Hatherly, 2022) is integral to the evolution in the meaning of an audit. This encompasses assurance on ESG, sustainability, and climate change issues (Barbour, 2022; Elkins et al., 2024; Erin & Ackers, 2024). Other aspects of assurance include internal control assurance, environmental auditing, privacy audits, non-GAAP earnings, cybersecurity risks, and integrated assurance (Hay, 2019; Jones, 2003). Again, it seems that the profession has been more concerned with maintaining a larger breadth of non-audit services than with redefining degrees of assurance. "Auditors will undoubtedly be increasingly asked to provide assurance over more subjective information, and only time will tell whether the current levels of assurance (reasonable and limited) will continue to meet the needs of users" (Barbour, 2022).

## Leveraging Technology for Comprehensive Audits

While many auditors might contest this, technological advancements could enable auditors to test not just a significantly larger portion of the population, but potentially the entire population throughout an audit period (Barandi et al., 2020; Kend & Nguyen, 2020). Full population testing is, arguably, becoming increasingly feasible due to advances in technology, powerful DA tools, and the increased use of AI and machine learning (Huang et al., 2022). This could incentivize auditors to overcome the limitations of traditional sampling by significantly increasing the sample size, potentially even testing the entire population.

However, the sheer volume of data and transactions still poses a challenge. Huang et al. (2022) illustrate this with the example of auditing a company like Amazon, which delivers billions of packages annually. With close to 15 million packages delivered daily, how can any sample truly be representative? The authors suggest that the quality of audit evidence collected through traditional sampling in such cases is low. They propose that full population testing through "audit-by-exception" and "exceptional exceptions" would enhance audit findings using audit DA. The core idea is that auditors need to rethink auditing beyond traditional processes, where traditional sampling has been a prominent feature.

## Adapting to New Accounting Principles

There have also been proposals to shift auditing toward "new generally accepted accounting principles for the information age, to replace the accounting model of the industrial age" (PwC, 2000). Accordingly, the profile of the professional auditor is expected to evolve to address such a transformation (Barbour, 2022). Technological advancements are reshaping the role of professional auditors and the skills they need to acquire (Jackson & Allen, 2024). Auditors will increasingly need to use higher-order thinking skills, which will ultimately enhance audit quality (Moffitt et al., 2018). They will need to rely more on their discretion rather than solely on programmed technical abilities (Tiberius & Hirth, 2019). This shift will require additional training in areas beyond their traditional skill sets, such as business acumen, technology, and enhanced soft skills (Barbour, 2022). Hatherly (2022) anticipates the emergence of a new "super-auditor" in the future. This concept is intriguing because, if adopted, it may widen the audit expectations gap. Additionally, auditors must be more open to alternatives to the current partnership model of organizing and governing their firms (Hay, 2019).

### Overcoming Institutional Inertia

Big accounting firms need to be aware of institutional inertia and the various factors that contribute to it in order to act as institutional entrepreneurs. In an early essay on resistance within the profession, Smith (1958) noted that "any organized profession includes resistance to change within its very principles of organization; it possesses institutional inertia." Professional organizations, which have long been significant players on the national stage, are now highly organized globally. These organizations often serve as the "conscience of the community," making "best practice" recommendations (Brunsson et al., 2000). Greenwood et al. (2002) assert that professional organizations can foster a change-oriented discourse by initiating transformative discussions within the profession and then redefining professional identities for external communication. Given their substantial influence on syndicates and professional groups, big accounting firms can and should lead in this respect from a moral perspective.

## CONCLUSION

The auditing profession has been slow to evolve due to vested interests, outdated learning models, and a commitment to traditional approaches, resulting in institutional inertia and making transformational change difficult. Accounting firms frequently resist reforms and lobby to limit new regulations they deem counterproductive. One change that happened over the years, however, was the profession's shifting emphasis from public interest to a focus on profit and client commitment, often creating cultures where commercial interests take precedence. This shift aimed to align with market demands and attract young talent.

While the profession risks becoming too commercially focused, a complete shift in the opposite direction could revive the "boring accountant" stereotype, reducing interest in the field. On the other hand, a purely market-based perspective could trap the profession in a profit-seeking mindset. A balance must be struck, and institutional entrepreneurs need to lead this effort.

Institutional entrepreneurs – individuals or firms capable of driving substantial change – are crucial for this transformation. Big accounting firms, with their resources and influence, are well-positioned to act as these entrepreneurs but often seem reluctant. Their willingness to drive significant change remains uncertain. In all cases, they need to foster constructive organizational cultures and lead the process of "reimagining auditing." Institutional entrepreneurs play a significant role in shaping the identity of professional accountants, often more effectively than professional bodies and educational institutions.

# 5

# BRIDGING THE GAP: REIMAGINING AUDITING FOR THE FUTURE

*The current audit is valuable but needs to change...*

*Forbes Insights (n.d.)*

In an ideal world, there would be no audit expectations gap; the audit system would function flawlessly, and the audit profession would prosper. Regrettably, the ongoing debate about the persistent gap serves as a continual reminder of the various ailments afflicting the audit profession. A bigger difference in expectations leads to reduced credibility, lower confidence in the auditing profession, and a decline in the degree of prestige associated with an auditor's job. As a result, it is critical that the audit profession, together with other stakeholders, investigates further approaches to narrow the gap.

Failure to address the expectations gap would only compound the audit profession's present issues. Indeed, there are no signs that the audit expectations gap will be phased out soon. If anything, advancements in auditors' technology skills, which improve their capacity to broaden and deepen the breadth and complexity of their work, may increase rather than diminish the gap. Stakeholders who are aware of the influence of new technologies may be convinced even more that auditors can perform things that were previously impossible. The most recent improvement in AI capabilities may also worsen rather than close the gap.

Reimagining auditing requires imagining not only a whole profession but also the people behind it. This concluding chapter explores the meaning of "reimagining auditing" and what a novel approach would contribute to the profession and to business in general. The process of reimagining auditing necessitates the training of new auditors proficient in a distinct audit style. Related to that, this transformation requires change at multiple levels. We're going to address just three of those levels, specifically auditors themselves, the role of universities and the educational sector in advancing a new type of auditor, and the role of the profession itself. We present the roles of these three parties in terms of a tripartite model: **ACE** (the auditor) – **PLACE** (the university or the educational institution), and – **EMBRACE** (the profession) – Fig. 5.1.

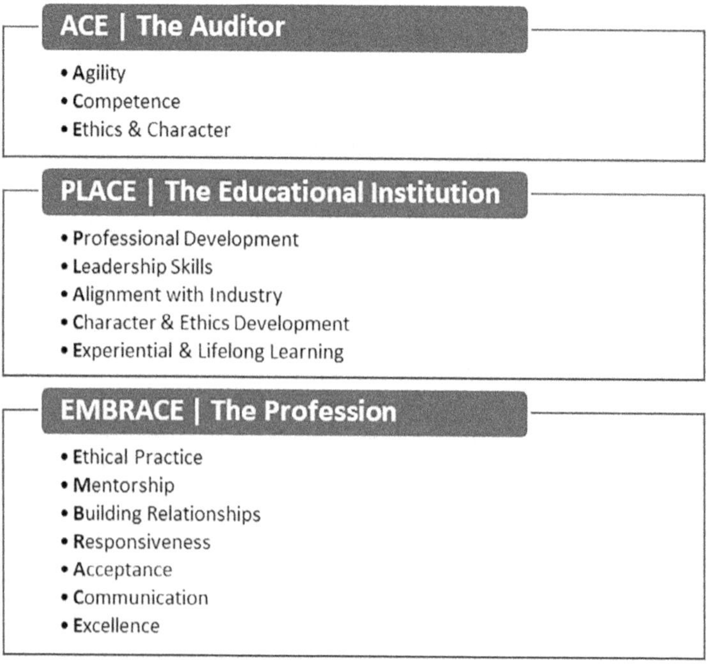

### ACE | The Auditor
- Agility
- Competence
- Ethics & Character

### PLACE | The Educational Institution
- Professional Development
- Leadership Skills
- Alignment with Industry
- Character & Ethics Development
- Experiential & Lifelong Learning

### EMBRACE | The Profession
- Ethical Practice
- Mentorship
- Building Relationships
- Responsiveness
- Acceptance
- Communication
- Excellence

**Fig. 5.1. Reimagining Auditing: A Tripartite Model.**

## ACE: THE FUTURE AUDITOR, AGILE, COMPETENT, AND ETHICAL

Reimagining auditing requires a new type of auditor. While not entirely different from existing auditors, this new type must possess additional competencies and skills. Auditors still need basic training in accounting and auditing principles, along with growing expertise. However, new skills, knowledge sets, abilities, competencies, and attitudes must complement this education and experience.

There is a growing interest in developing auditors who can master skills suited to the information age and digital transformation (Azizul Islam, 2017; BDO USA, n.d.; CLIMB, 2022; Farrel & Paquette, 2023; KPMG Insights, 2018; Teal HQ, n.d.; Thomson Reuters Tax & Accounting, 2024; Trullion, 2024). This is crucial, but there is more to do beyond improving technical skills. It is important to nurture the right mindsets and attitudes. Auditors must strive to excel in these areas, summarized by the ACE acronym: agility (A), competence (C), and ethical grounding and character (E).

### A: Agility

The auditing profession needs to be more adaptive and willing to change. For the profession to be agile, auditors themselves must be agile. They need to thrive in constantly changing environments, demonstrating flexibility in adapting to new contexts and technologies. Auditors must solve problems and work on complex projects, emphasizing teamwork and collaboration with professionals from various fields. Essential skills include navigating artificial intelligence, machine learning, blockchain technology, remote auditing, and robotic process automation.

### C: Competence

Competence involves having the skills and knowledge to perform well. Traditionally, this includes understanding accounting and auditing mechanics, business acumen, and other necessary skills.

However, the required competencies have expanded to include compliance issues, evolving reporting standards, regulatory knowledge, and cybersecurity. Auditors must also understand data management, analysis, and interrogation methodologies. There is a growing need for expertise in non-financial standards, such as ESG. According to an IFAC report, "professional accountants will need the skills to provide more all-inclusive corporate reporting, which tells less about the numbers and more about the narrative of the organization" (Azizul Islam, 2017). Auditors must also adapt to changes in smart and digital technology, globalization of accounting and auditing standards, and new aspects of regulation.

## E: Ethical Grounding & Character

Auditors must develop a strong ethical foundation and character, understanding what is right and acting accordingly. This requires training in ethical judgment, professional skepticism, moral sensitivity, imagination, judgment, motivation, courage, and engagement in moral behavior. Auditors should demonstrate a commitment to values and principles, not just displaying a concern about meeting budgets and deadlines.

## PLACE: EDUCATIONAL INSTITUTIONS – SCHOOLS OF BUSINESS

The second level of reimagining auditing involves the role of education, including schools of accounting and business, such as universities, corporate universities, and vocational schools. Educational institutions and professional bodies need to reflect and converse on how to best update and enhance their educational offerings. Previously, the focus of learning about accounting and auditing was on mastering the mechanics and technicalities of bookkeeping and auditing. Some university curricula have delved into specific areas of accounting and auditing to equip auditors with the necessary educational background for various industries and circumstances.

According to Gilbert (2005), external providers of resources affect and restrict a firm's strategic options. These external suppliers include educational and professional training organizations that develop auditors. Despite the expansion of talent attraction tools and profiles by global accounting firms, the career path of a typical certified auditor in many international jurisdictions has not fundamentally changed over the last few decades. It is crucial for colleges and other educational institutions, as well as the audit profession itself, to assess this in the context of the proposed paradigm shift and the need for reconstructed professional identities.

This change in perspective within the audit profession requires the implementation of new features in audit education and training. For example, auditors would need more training on the psychological traps they may fall into. This would involve thorough conversations with institutions that train future auditors, such as universities, to update and expand their educational offerings, reaffirming duties to a broader set of stakeholders. Prior research has shown that modifications in accounting curricula have been slow and ineffective in numerous ways (DiGabriele, 2016).

Auditors require training not only in advanced technological tools that improve audit work and efficiency but also in recognizing psychological traps. In addition to cultivating technically skilled junior auditors, educational institutions have the potential to foster the development of future auditors who possess a deep understanding of decision-making processes and are aware of the biases that might hinder sound judgment.

In addressing the role of educational institutions, we use the PLACE acronym.

## P: Professional Development

Developing the auditor's professional background remains a core objective of business schools. These institutions must continue to be the best source of accounting and auditing information while advancing the knowledge and skills of future auditors in emerging areas such as technology, compliance, changing regulations, and artificial intelligence.

### L: Leadership Skills

Beyond technical knowledge, there is an increasing need for auditors to be trained in soft skills, including leadership, negotiations, team management, and communication. Many practitioners and client companies emphasize these broader skill sets in today's environments.

### A: Alignment with Industry

Educational programs need to align with industry needs. Universities should engage with practitioner–mentors who can provide valuable feedback to aspiring auditors as they navigate their future workplaces. Business firms often have advanced insights into key issues facing practitioners; these should be integrated into the classroom. These need to take the shape of new courses into areas that accountants and auditors need to be aware of such as issues related to emerging technologies and AI.

### C: Character & Ethics Development

Ethics education should be a cornerstone of educational offerings. Institutions must decide whether to include an ethics dimension in each accounting and auditing class or to dedicate a whole course to business ethics. Accreditation agencies and auditor certification programs will not accept a curriculum that lacks business ethics education. This is increasingly becoming the benchmark for business and accounting education. Sidani (2023) linked the legitimacy of schools of business to their ability to graduate a "business citizen," the one who possesses the requisite skills, traits, and character to thrive in the real world:

> *schools of business need to repurpose business school education around developing the character of the total well-rounded business citizen, who is not a mere business professional. Success in doing that means that a school of business will remain relevant for generations to come (p. 230).*

### E: Experiential & Lifelong Learning

Curricula need to provide work experiences that closely mimic real life. This is increasingly feasible through more intense requirements for real-life experiences, internships, and training. The Association to Advance Collegiate Schools of Business (AACSB), a global organization that accredits business schools, notes that "business schools can provide greater value to companies by designing experiential opportunities for students to hone soft skills, cultivate professionalism, develop ethical foundations, and discover their sense of purpose." (Bisoux, 2024). Experiential learning develops a level of maturity that traditional classroom teaching cannot achieve (Lombardi et al., 2015).

## EMBRACE – THE PROFESSION (ETHICAL PRACTICE, MENTORSHIP, BUILDING RELATIONSHIPS, RESPONSIVENESS, ACCEPTANCE, COMMUNICATION, EXCELLENCE)

Earlier chapters have dwelled on the institutional mechanisms by which institutional inertia prevails impeding significant and meaningful change. There is a crucial need for the profession to reimagine auditing through institutional entrepreneurs. These leaders, with enough leverage and power, must EMBRACE change as follows:

### E: Ethical Practice

The profession needs to emphasize transparency, values, and ethics at every juncture. Despite advancements in integrating ethics into educational curricula and internal processes, there is still a need to uphold integrity and ethical standards by fostering ethical cultures. While the profession has advanced significantly over the last few decades following a series of corporate scandals and audit failures, there is still much that can be done. An important aspect of this comes through transformative efforts in organizational cultures. Traditionally, audit firms have focused on compliance-based cultures, where adherence to established regulations and policies is paramount. However, this approach is insufficient. There is a growing recognition of the importance of values-based cultures that emphasize principles over mere rules and values over mere compliance (Treviño et al., 1999; Tyler et al., 2008).

### M: Mentorship

Providing guidance and support to stakeholders is essential. The profession plays a significant role in knowledge transfer, leadership development, the inculcation of ethics and values, role modeling, enhancing professional relationships and networking, and instilling a spirit of professionalism over a spirit of pure commercialism. Mentorship is also a crucial aspect of career guidance, helping young auditors navigate their work and make pertinent career choices.

### B: Building Relationships

Reimagining auditing involves not only auditors rethinking their roles and professional duties but also other stakeholders understanding what auditing entails. This can be enhanced through auditors taking a leading role in fostering relationships with other stakeholders. The profession needs to strengthen relationships not only with clients but also with regulators, media, and educational institutions. Addressing the expectations gap requires negotiation between relevant parties, considering the cost–benefit analysis of audit work (Lee, 1994). Studies emphasize the need to educate the public about the nature of auditors' work and mitigate exaggerated responses to isolated auditing mishaps (Gay et al., 1998). This includes better explanations of the assurance process and the role of auditors (Haniffa & Hudaib, 2007). This dialog must be inclusive of various stakeholders to achieve better convergence on the "meaning of audit."

### R: Responsiveness

The audit profession needs to be responsive and adaptive to new challenges and opportunities. It must adopt new perspectives on what auditing means and what the profession needs to do to move forward. The profession should not stick to existing routines but embrace new ones. As discussed in earlier chapters, this requires a process of deinstitutionalizing old practices and legitimizing new ones. Auditors need to abandon the profession's long-standing defensive posture. The profession must be more proactive, particularly when faced with corporate failures partially attributed to auditors' actions or negligence. It should be more sensitive to major shocks impacting it and not just resort to defensive reflexes.

## A: Acceptance

Change is inevitable, and the auditing profession needs to accept the notion that it needs to evolve. It is also essential to acknowledge that the auditing profession cannot transform itself through internal discussions alone. It is crucial to engage with stakeholders and be open to depart from the traditional role the profession has been locked into. Being open to the idea that an auditor's role might change and that the public has increasing expectations of auditors is a step in the right direction. There also needs to be an acceptance to the notion that with technological advancements and AI tools, the public expectations of auditors may further increase.

## C: Communication

Ensuring clear and effective communication with stakeholders is crucial. Better communication is an important vehicle to narrow the expectations gap (Green & Li, 2012). For example, there is a need to clarify the language in audit reports (Cohen & Knechel, 2013; Mock et al., 2013). Auditors need to improve their communication techniques (Glover & Reidenbach, 2011) and better relate the level of assurance and the scope of work conducted (Gay et al., 1998). This would entail better training for auditors (Cohen & Knechel, 2013; Ruhnke & Schmidt, 2014; Wolf et al., 1999).

The expectations gap would also be narrowed if the legitimacy of auditors is increased, which becomes more possible when the value that auditors provide is made clear to users (D'Onza et al.,

2015). Public awareness about the role of auditors must be consistently promoted (Chen et al., 2012), and relevant stakeholders need to be educated and trained about the true boundaries of the auditing function (Noghondari & Foong, 2009). This education can help reduce the expectations gap by making the public aware that some of their expectations are unrealistic.

## E: Excellence

Striving for continuous improvement and excellence in all activities is essential. The business environment is changing at an increasing pace, bringing greater demands on auditors and the audit profession. The audit expectations gap can only be reduced if auditors and other stakeholders step up to the challenge and address the immense changes occurring in their environments that significantly impact how they do business and how they need to approach their audits. Collaborative work among academics and audit professionals, in tandem with other stakeholders, can help achieve the mutual objective of closing the gap and advancing the audit profession.

## CONCLUSION

The expectations gap has been a persistent issue in the auditing profession for many years. The persistence of this gap has been challenging for the profession, as constant public criticism has forced it to reconsider its value to society. The profession has not sufficiently mitigated the gap due to its desire to protect itself, failure to evolve, and institutional inertia. The profession should embrace the necessity of reimagining auditing (Citron, 2003), reconsidering its scope, users' perceptions of it, and identifying necessary adjustments to better meet the expectations of diverse stakeholders.

This requires auditors to recognize the existence of institutional inertia, understand its causes, and develop strategies to reconfigure the profession in terms of role, image, and identity. This necessitates bold institutional entrepreneurship, best undertaken by organizations with the legacy, authority, and resources to drive such change. Collaborative efforts among academics, audit professionals, and other stakeholders can help achieve the shared goal of closing the expectations gap and advancing the audit profession.

At the core of this change is a renewed emphasis on the ethical grounding of an audit, ethical education by universities and educational entities, and ethical practice by audit professionals. Fundamental and transformative change will only happen if professionals strike the right balance between being auditors who provide significant and valuable service to the public and paying attention to the well-being of firms and their various stakeholders. Auditing is not just another activity to sell a service; it is the foundation on which a sound economic and financial system can be built. Without auditors understanding their true role, reimagining the profession will not happen. The advancement of the profession will rest on those institutional entrepreneurs with the moral courage to elevate this profession upward and onward. Those individuals will build a future where auditing not only upholds integrity but also inspires trust and confidence in the financial systems that support our society.

# ABOUT THE AUTHORS

**Yusuf M. Sidani** (PhD, CPA) is a Professor of Leadership and Business Ethics at the Suliman S. Olayan School of Business, American University of Beirut (AUB), and is currently the Dean of the school. He also holds an MBA in accounting from Indiana University and is a Certified Public Accountant. His research focuses on leadership, with contributions in the fields of auditing and tax evasion. His work has appeared in leading international peer-reviewed academic journals.

**Tarek El Masri** (PhD, Certified Internal Auditor) is Assistant Professor of Accounting at the Prince Mohammed Bin Salman College (MBSC) of Business & Entrepreneurship. He has PhD from John Molson School of Business, Concordia University, Montreal, Canada. He researches topics related to corporate governance, with a particular focus on family firms, board of directors' composition, top management team compensation, gender diversity on boards, and ownership distribution. His research has won several awards in Canada, such as the National Bank Initiative in Entrepreneurship and Family Business Award and the Bell Research Centre – Scholarship Award. His practical work experience spans diverse institutions in Canada, Lebanon, Kuwait, and Saudi Arabia. He is a Member of the Beta Gamma Sigma academic honor society.

**Abdeljalil Ghanem** (PhD) is a Senior Lecturer in Accounting at the Suliman S. Olayan School of Business (AUB). Previously, he was a Financial Controller and company representative in the UAE for the SAUDI OGER/BELBADI group of companies and a Senior Auditor at DELOITTE & TOUCHE, SABA & CO international firm. At Bordeaux University in France, he specialized in Accounting and was awarded a PhD for his thesis on the

"Implementation of Accounting Valuation Models/Methods for an Industrial Company Planning Its Privatization." He has published research papers related to valuation, banking regulation, corporate governance, and tax evasion.

# REFERENCES

AbdulGaniyy, A. (2013). Audit practice in global perspective: Present and future challenges. *Research Journal of Finance and Accounting*, 4(6), 1–5.

Abiola, J. O. (2015). Audit expectation gap: Auditors in unending role conflict? *International Journal of Development and Management Review*, 10(1), 156–165.

ACCA. (2019, May 9). *Closing the expectation gap in audit*. Professional insight report. https://www.accaglobal.com/in/en/professional-insights/global-profession/expectation-gap.html

ACRA-ACCA. (2012). *Talent attraction and retention in larger accounting firms*. ACCA Global. https://www.accaglobal.com/content/dam/acca/global/PDF-technical/other-PDFs/talent-attraction-singapore.pdf

AICPA. (1948). *Professional standards, code of professional ethics, rule 8*. American Institute of Certified Public Accountants.

AICPA. (1973). *Code of professional ethics rule 5.02*. American Institute of Certified Public Accountants.

AICPAs. (2023). *Consideration of fraud in a financial statement audit: AU-C 240*. American Institute of Certified Public Accountants.

Aksom, H. (2022). Institutional inertia and practice variation. *Journal of Organizational Change Management*, 35(3), 463–487.

Akther, T., & Xu, F. (2020). Existence of the audit expectation gap and its impact on stakeholders' confidence: The moderating role of the Financial Reporting Council. *International Journal of Financial Studies*, 8(1), 1–25.

Alexeyeva, I., & Svanström, T. (2015). The impact of the global financial crisis on audit and non-audit fees: Evidence from Sweden. *Managerial Auditing Journal*, 30(4/5), 302–323.

Ali, F., Aamir, M., Arz Bhutto, S., & Mubeen, M. (2015). A review and identification of aspects that contribute towards creation of audit expectation gap, a step towards narrowing this gap. *Developing Countries Studies*, 5(11), 29–39.

Allam, A., Ghattas, N., Kotb, A., & Eldaly, M. K. (2017). Audit tendering in the UK: A review of stakeholders' views. *International Journal of Auditing*, 21(1), 11–23.

Alleyne, P., & Howard, M. (2005). An exploratory study of auditors' responsibility for fraud detection in Barbados. *Managerial Auditing Journal*, 20(3), 284–303.

Alvin Alleyne, P., Devonish, D., & Alleyne, P. (2006). Perceptions of auditor independence in Barbados. *Managerial Auditing Journal*, 21(6), 621–635.

Anderson, U. (2000). *Summary of intended public testimony re: S7-13-00*. https://www.sec.gov/rules/proposed/s71300/testimony/anderso1.htm

Aobdia, D., Enache, L., & Srivastava, A. (2016). *Is the auditing industry becoming a tighter or looser oligopoly?* Tuck school of business working paper (2643862).

Atkinson, K. E., & Jones, R. C. (2014). The history and structure of the auditing profession from 1975 through 1990. *International Research Journal of Applied Finance*, 5(3), 329–338.

Attahiru, M. S., Al-Aidaros, A. H., & Yusof, S. B. M. (2016). Moderating role of Hisbah Institution on the relationship of religiosity and Islamic culture to Islamic work ethics in Nigeria. *International Review of Management and Marketing*, 6(8), 125–132.

Austin, A. A. (2023). Remembering fraud in the future: Investigating and improving auditors' attention to fraud during audit testing. *Contemporary Accounting Research*, 40(2), 925–951.

Awadallah, E. (2018). Auditor-client negotiations: Applying the dual concerns model in an emerging economy. *International Journal of Managerial and Financial Accounting*, 10(3), 250–272.

Azizul Islam, M. (2017, February 10). *Future of the accounting profession: Three major changes and implications for teaching and research*. IFAC. https://www.ifac.org/knowledge-gateway/discussion/future-accounting-profession-three-major-changes-and-implications-teaching-and-research

Baker, C. R. (1993). Self-regulation in the public accounting profession: The structural response of the large public accounting firms to a changing environment. *Accounting, Auditing & Accountability Journal, 6*(2), 68–80.

Barandi, Z., Lawson-Body, A., Lawson-Body, L., & Willoughby, L. (2020). Impact of blockchain technology on continuous auditing: Mediating role of transaction cost theory. *Issues in Information Systems, 21*(2), 206–2012.

Barbour, J. E. (2022). The future of audit: A personal perspective. *International Journal of Auditing, 26*(1), 4–7.

Baron, C. D., Johnson, D. A., Searfoss, D. G., & Smith, C. H. (1977). Uncovering corporate irregularities: Are we closing the expectation gap? *Journal of Accountancy, 144*(4), 56–66.

Battilana, J., Leca, B., & Boxenbaum, E. (2009). How actors change institutions: Towards a theory of institutional entrepreneurship. *Academy of Management Annals, 3*(1), 65–107

Bazerman, M. H., & Moore, D. (2011). Is it time for auditor independence yet? *Accounting, Organizations and Society, 36*(4–5), 310–312.

Bazerman, M. H., & Moore, D. A. (2012). *Judgment in managerial decision making* (8th ed.). John Wiley & Sons.

Bazerman, M. H., Morgan, K. P., & Loewenstein, G. F. (1997). The impossibility of auditor independence. *MIT Sloan Management Review, 38*(Summer), 89–94.

BDO USA. (n.d.). *The future of the audit in 5 predictions*. BDO. https://www.bdo.com/insights/assurance/the-future-of-the-audit-in-5-predictions

Bedard, J. C., Sutton, S. G., Arnold, V., & Phillips, J. R. (2012). Another piece of the "expectations gap": What do investors know about auditor involvement with information in the annual report? *Current Issues in Auditing, 6*(1), A17–A30.

Betti, N., DeSimone, S., Gray, J., & Poncin, I. (2024). The impacts of the use of data analytics and the performance of consulting activities on perceived internal audit quality. *Journal of Accounting & Organizational Change*, 20(2), 334–361.

Bierman, H. (2013). The 1929 stock market crash. In *Routledge handbook of major events in economic history* (pp. 119–126). Routledge.

Billard, O., Ivaldi, M., & Mitraille, S. (2011). Evaluation of the risks of collective dominance in the audit industry in France. *European Competition Journal*, 7(2), 349–378.

Bisoux, T. (2024, March). *What can business schools and industry do together?* AACSB Insights. https://www.aacsb.edu/insights/articles/2024/03/what-can-business-schools-and-industry-do-together#:~:text=Business%20schools%20can%20provide%20greater,discover%20their%20sense%20of%20purpose

Blood, B., & Yong, J. (2024, March 20). *Addressing the decline in the accounting talent pipeline.* International Federation of Accountants. https://www.ifac.org/knowledge-gateway/discussion/addressing-decline-accounting-talent-pipeline

Bohne, R. (2024, May 22). *Revenue of the Big Four accounting/audit firms worldwide in 2023.* Statista. https://www.statista.com/statistics/250479/big-four-accounting-firms-global-revenue/

Bohne, R. (2025). Number of employees of the Big Four accounting/audit firms worldwide in 2024. Statista. https://www.statista.com/statistics/250503/big-four-accounting-firms-number-of-employees/

Boo, K. (2023, March 20). Deloitte to add 3,000 new hires in Singapore within five years to boost accountancy sector. *The Straits Times*. https://www.straitstimes.com/business/deloitte-to-add-3000-new-hires-in-s-pore-within-five-years-to-boost-accountancy-sector.

Broberg, P., Umans, T., Skog, P., & Theodorsson, E. (2018). Auditors' professional and organizational identities and commercialization in audit firms. *Accounting, Auditing & Accountability Journal*, 31(2), 374–399.

Brunsson, N., Jacobsson, B., & Associates. (2000). *A world of standards.* Oxford University Press.

# References

Buddery, P., Frank, S., & Martinoff, M. (2014). *Enlightening professions? A vision for audit and a better society*. Audit Futures & RSA.

Burnett, B., Chen, H., & Gunny, K. (2018). Auditor-provided lobbying service and audit quality. *Journal of Accounting, Auditing & Finance*, 33(3), 402–434.

Cadiz Dyball, M., & Valcarcel, L. J. (1999). The "rational" and "traditional": The regulation of accounting in the Philippines. *Accounting, Auditing & Accountability Journal*, 12(3), 303–328.

Cameron, K. S., & Quinn, R. E. (2005). *Diagnosing and changing organizational culture: Based on the competing values framework*. John Wiley & Sons.

Capriotti, R. J. (2014). Big data: Bringing big changes to accounting. *Pennsylvania CPA Journal*, 85(2), 36–38.

Carlozo, L. (2017). Why CPAs need to get a grip on blockchain. *Journal of Accountancy*. https://www.journalofaccountancy.com/news/2017/jun/blockchain-decentralized-ledger-system201716738.html

Cassell, C. A., Dearden, S. M., Rosser, D. M., & Shipman, J. E. (2022). Confirmation bias and auditor risk assessments: Archival evidence. *Auditing: A Journal of Practice & Theory*, 41(3), 67–93.

Chandler, R., & Edwards, J. R. (1996). Recurring issues in auditing: Back to the future? *Accounting, Auditing & Accountability Journal*, 9(2), 4–29.

Chen, J. H. (2024). When employees go to court: Employee lawsuits and talent acquisition in audit offices. *Journal of Accounting Research*, 62(4), 1265–1307. https://doi.org/10.xxxx/jar.2024.xxxx

Chen, L., Jones, K. L., Lisic, L. L., Michas, P., Pawlewicz, R., & Pevzner, M. B. (2012). Comments by the Auditing Standards Committee of the Auditing Section of the American Accounting Association on the IAASB Proposal: Improving the auditor's report: Participating committee members and other contributors. *Current Issues in Auditing*, 7(1), C11–C20.

Chesser, D. L., Moore, C. W., & Conway, L. G. (1994). Has advertising by CPA's promoted a trend toward commercialism? *Journal of Applied Business Research*, 10(2), 98–105.

Christensen, B. E., Glover, S. M., & Wood, D. A. (2012). Extreme estimation uncertainty in fair value estimates: Implications for audit assurance. *Auditing: A Journal of Practice & Theory, 31*(1), 127–146.

Christensen, M., & Rocher, S. (2020). The persistence of accountant beancounter images in popular culture. *Accounting, Auditing & Accountability Journal, 33*(6), 1395–1422.

Chui, L., Curtis, M. B., & Pike, B. J. (2022). How does an audit or a forensic perspective influence auditors' fraud-risk assessment and subsequent risk response? *Auditing: A Journal of Practice & Theory, 41*(4), 57–83.

Chye Koh, H., & Woo, E. S. (1998). The expectation gap in auditing. *Managerial Auditing Journal, 13*(3), 147–154.

Citron, D. B. (2003). The UK's framework approach to auditor independence and the commercialization of the accounting profession. *Accounting, Auditing & Accountability Journal, 16*(2), 244–274.

CLIMB. (2022, August 5). *16 external auditor skills for your career and resume*. CLIMB. https://climbtheladder.com/external-auditor-skills/

Coffee, J. C. (2019). Why do auditors fail? What might work? What won't? *Accounting and Business Research, 49*(5), 540–561.

Cohen Commission. (1978). *The commission on auditors' responsibilities: Report, conclusions, and recommendations*. AICPA.

Cohen, J. R., & Knechel, W. R. (2013). A call for academic inquiry: Challenges and opportunities from the PCAOB synthesis projects. *Auditing: A Journal of Practice & Theory, 32*(sp1), 1–5.

Cohen, J., Ding, Y., Lesage, C., & Stolowy, H. (2017). Media bias and the persistence of the expectation gap: An analysis of press articles on corporate fraud. *Journal of Business Ethics, 144*(3), 637–659.

Congress. (2002). *H.R.3763 – Sarbanes-Oxley Act of 2002*. https://www.congress.gov/bill/107th-congress/house-bill/3763

Cooper, D. J., & Robson, K. (2006). Accounting, professions and regulation: Locating the sites of professionalization. *Accounting, Organizations and Society, 31*(4–5), 415–444.

# References

Coram, P. J., & Wang, L. (2021). The effect of disclosing key audit matters and accounting standard precision on the audit expectation gap. *International Journal of Auditing*, 25(2), 270–282.

Cornell, R. M., Eining, M. M., & Warne, R. C. (2012). Practitioner summary of can auditors reduce negligence verdicts? An examination of remedial tactics. *Current Issues in Auditing*, 6(2), P1–P6.

Daher, K. (2020, February 23). Responsibility of board members and auditors. *Al-Akhbar*. https://al-akhbar.com/Issues/284583

Daoust, L. (2020). Playing the Big Four recruitment game: The tension between illusio and reflexivity. *Critical Perspectives on Accounting*, 66, 102081.

Daoust, L., & Malsch, B. (2019). How ex-auditors remember their past: The transformation of audit experience into cultural memory. *Accounting, Organizations and Society*, 77, 101050.

DeCoster, D. T., & Rhode, J. G. (1971). The accountant's stereotype: Real or imagined, deserved or unwarranted. *The Accounting Review*, 46(4), 651–664.

Deegan, C. (2002). Introduction: The legitimising effect of social and environmental disclosures – A theoretical foundation. *Accounting, Auditing & Accountability Journal*, 15(3), 282–311.

Deloitte. (n.d). *Frontpage*. Deloitte Global. https://www.deloitte.com/global/en.html

Dermarkar, S., & Hazgui, M. (2022). How auditors legitimize commercialism: A micro-discursive analysis. *Critical Perspectives on Accounting*, 83, 1–20.

DiGabriele, J. A. (2016). The expectation differences among stakeholders in the financial valuation fitness of auditors. *Journal of Applied Accounting Research*, 17(1), 43–60.

Diolas, A. (2024). *Attract, engage, retain: Insights and recommendations for audit talent success*. ACCA Global.

Dogarawa, A. B. (2013). Hisbah and the promotion of ethical business practices: A reflection for the Shari'ah implementing states in Nigeria.

*International Journal of Islamic and Middle Eastern Finance and Management, 6*(1), 51–63.

Donn, N. (2018, April 17). Bank of Portugal blames auditors for BES debacle. *Portugal Resident.* https://www.portugalresident.com/bank-of-portugal-blames-auditors-for-bes-debacle/

D'Onza, G., Lamboglia, R., & Verona, R. (2015). Do IT audits satisfy senior manager expectations? A qualitative study based on Italian banks. *Managerial Auditing Journal, 30*(4/5), 413–434.

Dunne, N. J., Brennan, N. M., & Kirwan, C. E. (2021). Impression management and Big Four auditors: Scrutiny at a public inquiry. *Accounting, Organizations and Society, 88,* 101170.

Eaglesham, J. (2022). Audit regulator steps up enforcement under new leader. *The Wall Street Journal.* https://www.wsj.com/articles/audit-regulator-steps-up-enforcement-under-new-leader-11666992637?mod=Searchresults_pos3&page=1

Earley, C. E. (2015). Data analytics in auditing: Opportunities and challenges. *Business Horizons, 58*(5), 493–500.

EC. (2011). IMPACT ASSESSMENT accompanying the document Proposal for a Directive of the European Parliament and of the Council amending Directive 2006/43/EC on statutory audits of annual accounts and consolidated accounts. *The European Commission*, Brussels, 30.11.2011.

Elayan, F. A., Brown, K., Pacharn, P., Chen, Y., & Li, J. (2024). *Auditee merger, audit fees, and the market dominance of Big Four accounting firms.* SSRN. https://doi.org/10.2139/ssrn.4700711

Elkins, H., Entwistle, G., & Schmidt, R. N. (2024). Expectations for sustainability reporting from users, preparers, and the accounting profession. *International Journal of Disclosure and Governance, 21*(2), 143–164.

Elliot, V. H. (2016). Institutional entrepreneurship and change: A contemporary history of the Swedish banking industry and its performance management systems. *Journal of Accounting & Organizational Change, 12*(2), 223–251.

Elshandidy, T., Eldaly, M. K., & Abdel-Kader, M. (2021). Independent oversight of the auditing profession: A review of the literature. *International Journal of Auditing*, 25(2), 373–407.

Erin, O. A., & Ackers, B. (2024). Corporate board, assurance and sustainability reporting practices: A focus on selected African countries. *Journal of Accounting & Organizational Change*, 20(6), 85–118.

Essex, D. (2018, July 16). Do auditors no longer put principle before profit? *The Financial Times*. https://www.ft.com/content/8ae5cf40-7886-11e8-bc55-50daf11b720d

EUR-Lex. (2014). *Regulation (EU) No 537/2014 of the European Parliament and of the council of 16 April 2014 on specific requirements regarding statutory audit*. European Union. https://eur-lex.europa.eu/legal-content/EN/TXT/?uri=CELEX%3A32014R0537

EY. (n.d.). *Frontpage*. Ernst & Young Global Limited. https://www.ey.com/en_lb

Farmer, T. A., Rittenberg, L. E., & Trompeter, G. M. (1987). An investigation of the impact of economic and organizational-factors on auditor independence. *Auditing: A Journal of Practice & Theory*, 7(1), 1–14.

Farrell, J., & Paquette, H. (2023, March 31). Get ready for the future of auditing. *The CPA Journal*. https://www.cpajournal.com/2023/03/31/get-ready-for-the-future-of-auditing/

Fathallah, R., Sidani, Y., & Khalil, S. (2020). How religion shapes family business ethical behaviors: An institutional logics perspective. *Journal of Business Ethics*, 163(4), 647–659.

FDIC. (2019, March 15). *FDIC settles with PricewaterhouseCoopers LLP on audits of a failed bank*. Federal Deposit Insurance Corporation. https://www.fdic.gov/news/press-releases/2019/pr19019.html

Fisher, D. (2017, March 23). PwC settles with MF Global, leaving question of auditor liability for another case. *Forbes*. https://www.forbes.com/sites/danielfisher/2017/03/23/pwc-settles-with-mf-global-leaving-question-of-auditor-liability-for-another-case/#6925735f1900

Flesher, D. L., Previts, G. J., & Samson, W. D. (2005). Auditing in the United States: A historical perspective. *Abacus*, 41(1), 21–39.

Flood, E. (2023, March 27). Talent shortage frustrates internal auditors. *CFO Dive*. https://www.cfodive.com/news/talent-shortage-frustrates-internal-auditors/646071/

Foley, S. (2024a, January 2). Big Four firms rethink governance after year of mis-steps and scandals. *The Financial Times*. https://www.ft.com/content/2442852f-69ac-4e87-ba6e-b16343654d83

Foley, S. (2024b, January 30). Top accounting firms admit breaking rules safeguarding audit independence. *The Financial Times*. https://www.ft.com/content/a3bdf4fc-151c-436f-aeb9-b5e9b4d60d23

Foley, S. (2024c, June 6). Alvarez & Marsal poaches from Big Four rivals in expansion push. *The Financial Times*. https://www.ft.com/content/6fa8edc1-bf3b-4753-8b0f-935440188e8e

Foley, S., & Foy, S. (2024, June 27). New EY chief rules out reviving plan to split Big Four firm in two. *The Financial Times*. https://www.ft.com/content/5532b2dd-c7b4-4d04-b433-2ad30052ebfb

Foley, S., & O'Dwyer, M. (2023, September 10). PwC to curtail consulting work for US audit clients to reduce conflict risk. *The Financial Times*. https://www.ft.com/content/a17644d8-bbef-4cca-bcb4-06ed14e59180

Forbes Insights. (n.d.). *Future role of audit: A more insightful audit for a more complex world*. https://images.forbes.com/forbesinsights/StudyPDFs/Insights_GPPC_REPORT.pdf

Francis, J. R. (2024). *Why regulate auditing? Externalities and the limits of regulation*. SSRN. https://ssrn.com/abstract=4951469 or http://dx.doi.org/10.2139/ssrn.4951469

Frank, M. L., & Hoffman, V. B. (2015). How audit reviewers respond to an audit preparer's affective bias: The ironic rebound effect. *The Accounting Review*, 90(2), 559–577.

FRC. (2018, June 18). *Big Four audit quality review results decline*. The Financial Reporting Council. https://www.frc.org.uk/news-and-events/news/2018/06/big-four-audit-quality-review-results-decline/

García Benau, M. A., & Humphrey, C. (1992). Beyond the audit expectations gap: Learning from the experiences of Britain and Spain. *European Accounting Review*, 1(2), 303–331.

# References

Gay, G., Schelluch, P., & Baines, A. (1998). Perceptions of messages conveyed by review and audit reports. *Accounting, Auditing & Accountability Journal*, 11(4), 472–494.

Gendron, Y., & Spira, L. F. (2010). Identity narratives under threat: A study of former members of Arthur Andersen. *Accounting, Organizations and Society*, 35(3), 275–300.

Gendron, Y., & Suddady, R. (2004). Professional insecurity and the erosion of accountancy's jurisdictional boundaries. *Canadian Accounting Perspectives*, 3(1), 85–115.

Gibassier, D., El Omari, S., & Naccache, P. (2020). Institutional work in the birth of a carbon accounting profession. *Accounting, Auditing & Accountability Journal*, 33(6), 1447–1476.

Gilbert, C. G. (2005). Unbundling the structure of inertia: Resource versus routine rigidity. *Academy of Management Journal*, 48(5), 741–763.

Glover, H. D., & Reidenbach, M. (2011). Auditor reporting model modifications: Practical insights from the academic community. *Current Issues in Auditing*, 6(1), C7–C14.

Green, W., & Li, Q. (2012). Evidence of an expectation gap for greenhouse gas emissions assurance. *Accounting, Auditing & Accountability Journal*, 25(1), 146–173.

Greenwood, R., Raynard, M., Kodeih, F., Micelotta, E. R., & Lounsbury, M. (2011). Institutional complexity and organizational responses. *Academy of Management Annals*, 5(1), 317–371.

Greenwood, R., Suddaby, R., & Hinings, C. R. (2002). Theorizing change: The role of professional associations in the transformation of institutionalized fields. *Academy of Management Journal*, 45(1), 58–80.

Groth, J. C., & Dye, R. T. (1999). Service quality: Perceived value, expectations, shortfalls, and bonuses. *Managing Service Quality: An International Journal*, 9(4), 274–286.

Guiral, A., Rodgers, W., Ruiz, E., & Gonzalo, J. A. (2010). Ethical dilemmas in auditing: Dishonesty or unintentional bias? *Journal of Business Ethics*, 91, 151–166.

Guiral, A., Rodgers, W., Ruiz, E., & Gonzalo-Angulo, J. A. (2015). Can expertise mitigate auditors' unintentional biases? *Journal of International Accounting, Auditing and Taxation*, 24, 105–117.

Haag, S. (2014). *Organizational inertia as barrier to firms' IT adoption*. Twentieth Americas Conference on Information Systems, Savannah.

Hamilton, S. E. (2013). Exploring professional identity: The perceptions of chartered accountant students. *The British Accounting Review*, 45(1), 37–49.

Hammond, T., & Sikka, P. (1996). Radicalizing accounting history: The potential of oral history. *Accounting, Auditing & Accountability Journal*, 9(3), 79–97.

Haniffa, R., & Hudaib, M. (2007). Locating audit expectations gap within a cultural context: The case of Saudi Arabia. *Journal of International Accounting, Auditing and Taxation*, 16(2), 179–206.

Hanlon, G., (1994). *The commercialisation of accountancy: Flexible accumulation and the transformation of the service class*. Macmillan.

Hannan, M. T., & Freeman, J. (1984). Structural inertia and organizational change. *American Sociological Review*, 49(2), 149–164.

Harber, M., & Willows, G. D. (2022). The commercialist identity of mid-tier firm auditors: A precarious balancing of priorities. *Accounting, Auditing & Accountability Journal*, 35(8), 1803–1829.

Harber, M., Maroun, W., & de Ricquebourg, A. D. (2023a). Audit firm executives under pressure: A discursive analysis of legitimisation and resistance to reform. *Critical Perspectives on Accounting*, 97. https://doi.org/10.1016/j.cpa.2023.102580

Harber, M., Verhoef, G., & de Villiers, C. (2023b). Disputed interpretations and active strategies of resistance during an audit regulatory debate. *Accounting, Auditing & Accountability Journal*, 36(2), 620–648.

Hardy, C., & Maguire, S. (2008). Institutional entrepreneurship. *The Sage Handbook of Organizational Institutionalism*, 1, 198–217.

Harris, S. (2018, July 3). Auditing watchdogs should remind the Big Four of their public duty. *The Financial Times*. https://www.ft.com/content/9a4fe61a-7eb6-11e8-af48-190d103e32a4

Hassink, H. F., Bollen, L. H., Meuwissen, R. H., & de Vries, M. J. (2009). Corporate fraud and the audit expectations gap: A study among business managers. *Journal of International Accounting, Auditing and Taxation*, *18*(2), 85–100.

Hatherly, D. (2022). The super-auditor, perpetual beta and pervasive performativity. *International Journal of Auditing*, *26*(1), 23–26.

Hay, D. (2019). *The future of auditing*. Routledge.

Henderson, C. M., Steinhoff, L., Harmeling, C. M., & Palmatier, R. W. (2021). Customer inertia marketing. *Journal of the Academy of Marketing Science*, *49*, 350–373.

Holm, C., & Zaman, M. (2012, March). Regulating audit quality: Restoring trust and legitimacy. *Accounting Forum*, *36*(1), 51–61.

Holtzman, Y. (2004). The transformation of the accounting profession in the United States: From information processing to strategic business advising. *Journal of Management Development*, *23*(10), 949–961.

Horton, J., Livne, G., & Pettinicchio, A. (2021). Empirical evidence on audit quality under a dual mandatory auditor rotation rule. *European Accounting Review*, *30*(1), 1–29.

Hossain, M., & Mitra, S. (2022). Do auditors account for firm-level political risk? *International Journal of Auditing*, *26*(4), 534–552.

House of Commons. (2019, April). *The future of audit*. BEIS committee report [HC 1718]. https://publications.parliament.uk/pa/cm201719/cmselect/cmbeis/1718/1718.pdf

Howieson, B. (2013). Quis auditoret ipsos auditores? Can auditors be trusted?. *Australian Accounting Review*, *23*(4), 295–306.

HR Director. (2023, June 3). *Talent shortage in auditing spells dire consequences for global economy*. https://www.thehrdirector.com/talent-shortage-auditing-spells-dire-consequences-global-economy/

Huang, F., No, W. G., Vasarhelyi, M. A., & Yan, Z. (2022). Audit data analytics, machine learning, and full population testing. *The Journal of Finance and Data Science*, *8*, 138–144.

Humphrey, C., & Moizer, P. (1990). From techniques to ideologies: An alternative perspective on the audit function. *Critical Perspectives on Accounting*, 1(3), 217–238.

Humphrey, C., Loft, A., & Woods, M. (2009). The global audit profession and the international financial architecture: Understanding regulatory relationships at a time of financial crisis. *Accounting, Organizations and Society*, 34(6–7), 810–825.

Humphrey, C., Sonnerfeldt, A., Komori, N., & Curtis, E. (2021). Audit and the pursuit of dynamic repair. *European Accounting Review*, 30(3), 445–471.

Humphrey, C., Turley, S., & Moizer, P. (1993). Protecting against detection: The case of auditors and fraud? *Accounting, Auditing & Accountability Journal*, 6(1), 39–62.

ICAEW. (n.d.). *Steps to a professional body – A timeline of the development of the Accountancy Profession in the United Kingdom*. The Institute of Chartered Accountants in England and Wales. https://www.icaew.com/library/historical-resources/timeline

ICAEW. (2021, January). *I don't want an auditor who is dynamic and creative. I want somebody I can trust*. ICAEW Insights. https://www.icaew.com/insights/viewpoints-on-the-news/2021/jan-2021/i-dont-want-a-creative-auditor-i-want-one-i-can-trust

ICAEW Insights. (2023, February 27). *What's creating the talent shortage?* ICAEW. https://www.icaew.com/insights/viewpoints-on-the-news/2023/feb-2023/whats-creating-the-talent-shortage

IFAC. (2018a). *IFAC & global accountancy profession urge G20 to prioritize sustainability and governance*. International Federation of Accountants. https://www.ifac.org/news-events/2024-10/ifac-global-accountancy-profession-urge-g20-prioritize-sustainability-and-governance

IFAC. (2018b). *Global accounting ethics & audit standards achieving worldwide adoption*. International Federation of Accountants. https://www.ifac.org/news-events/2018-04/global-accounting-ethics-audit-standards-achieving-worldwide-adoption

IFRS. (2023, September). *Analysis of the IFRS Accounting jurisdiction profiles*. International Financial Reporting Standards

Foundation. https://www.ifrs.org/use-around-the-world/use-of-ifrs-standards-by-jurisdiction/#analysis-of-the-168-profiles

Izza, M. (2019). 'Why do auditors fail? What might work? What won't?': A practitioner view. *Accounting and Business Research*, 49(5), 562–564.

Jackson, D., & Allen, C. (2024). Technology adoption in accounting: The role of staff perceptions and organisational context. *Journal of Accounting & Organizational Change*, 20(2), 205–227.

Jeacle, I. (2008). Beyond the boring grey: The construction of the colourful accountant. *Critical Perspectives on Accounting*, 19(8), 1296–1320.

Jenkins, P. (2013, December 13). Auditing watchdog slams 'below average' bank testing. *The Financial Times*. https://www.ft.com/content/0ec5693c-635c-11e3-886f-00144feabdc0

Jones, E. (1995). *True and fair: A history of price waterhouse*. Hamish Hamilton.

Jones, M. J. (2003). Accounting for biodiversity: Operationalising environmental accounting. *Accounting, Auditing & Accountability Journal*, 16(5), 762–789.

Jones, M. J. (2008). Internal control, accountability and corporate governance: Medieval and modern Britain compared. *Accounting, Auditing & Accountability Journal*, 21(7), 1052–1075.

Jones, M. J. (2009). Origins of medieval Exchequer accounting. *Accounting, Business & Financial History*, 19(3), 259–285.

Kao, J. (2023, December 11). Transcript: The Big Four's year of lay-offs. *The Financial Times*. https://www.ft.com/content/d53c809d-0606-4b52-8ad9-5b260a3ad7c2

Kassem, R. (2024). Beyond the numbers: Assessing the risk of management motives for fraud in external audits. *Journal of Accounting Literature*. https://doi.org/10.1108/JAL-02-2024-0018

Kells, S., & Gow, I. (2018, May 29). Ghosts of past frauds haunt the Big Four auditors (p. 1). *The Times*.

Kelly, J. (2018). *Message from Jack Kelly, head of audit quality & risk management* (p. 6). Deloitte 2018 transparency report. https://www2.

deloitte.com/content/dam/Deloitte/uk/Documents/about-deloitte/deloitte-uk-audit-transparency-report-2018.pdf

Kend, M., & Nguyen, L. A. (2020). Big data analytics and other emerging technologies: The impact on the Australian audit and assurance profession. *Australian Accounting Review*, *30*(4), 269–282.

Kesimli, I., Kesimli, & Achauer. (2019). *External auditing and quality*. Springer.

Khalil, E. L. (2013). Lock-in institutions and efficiency. *Journal of Economic Behavior & Organization*, *88*, 27–36.

Kinder, T. (2020, January 29). Decision looms over Big Four consultancy and audit 'conflict'. *The Financial Times*. https://www.ft.com/content/dfd5703a-2363-11ea-b8a1-584213ee7b2b

King, R. R. (2002). An experimental investigation of self-serving biases in an auditing trust game: The effect of group affiliation. *The Accounting Review*, *77*(2), 265–284.

King, D. L., & Case, C. J. (2016). A concise history of professional accounting associations. *ASBBS Proceedings*, *23*(1), 314.

Kingsley, S. (2018, January 15). Auditing's expectation gap is worse than ever. *Financial Times*. https://www.ft.com/content/a7a2cc56-f793-11e7-88f7-5465a6ce1a00

Kinney Jr, W. R., & Nelson, M. W. (1996). Outcome information and the "expectations gap": The case of loss contingencies. *Journal of Accounting Research*, *34*, 281–299.

Kohli, A. K., & Jaworski, B. J. (1990). Market orientation: The construct, research propositions, and managerial implications. *Journal of Marketing*, *54*(2), 1–18.

KPMG Insights. (2018, July 16). *Five skills auditors need to succeed today*. Forbes. https://www.forbes.com/sites/insights-kpmg/2018/07/16/five-skills-auditors-need-to-succeed-today/

Künneke, J., Grabner, I., & Moers, F. (2017). FAR research project: The loss of talent: A threat for audit quality? *Maandblad voor Accountancy en Bedrijfseconomie*, *91*(9/10), 268–273.

# References

LaGroue, L. E. (2014). *Accounting and auditing in Roman society* [Doctoral dissertation]. The University of North Carolina at Chapel Hill.

Lane, M. (2023). *Plato and the Idea of Political Office*. https://www.gresham.ac.uk/sites/default/files/transcript/2023-10-19-1800_Lane-T_0.pdf

Larson, M. S. (1977). *The rise of professionalism: A sociological analysis*. University of California Press.

Leão, F., & Gomes, D. (2022). The stereotype of accountants: Using a personality approach to assess the perspectives of laypeople. *Accounting, Auditing & Accountability Journal, 35*(9), 234–271.

Lee, T. (1994). Financial reporting quality labels: The social construction of the audit profession and the expectations gap. *Accounting, Auditing & Accountability Journal, 7*(2), 30–49.

Lee, T. A. (2011). Bankrupt accountants and lawyers: Transition in the rise of professionalism in Victorian Scotland. *Accounting, Auditing & Accountability Journal, 24*(7), 879–903.

Lee, T. A., Clarke, F. L., & Dean, G. W. (2020). Scandals. In J. R. Edwards, & S. P. Walker (Eds.). *The Routledge companion to accounting history* (pp. 408–429). Routledge.

Lehman, G. (2014). Moral will, accounting and the phronemos. *Critical Perspectives on Accounting, 25*(3), 210–216.

Leng, C., Ho-Him, C., Foley, S., & Foy, S. (2024, September 13). PwC banned for 6 months in China for 'concealing fraud' at Evergrande. *The Financial Times*. https://www.ft.com/content/f4e0a831-d738-4bb1-98f8-6cff6a27a1ed

Levy, H. B. (2020, November). History of the auditing world, Part 1. *The CPA Journal*. https://www.cpajournal.com/2020/11/25/history-of-the-auditing-world-part-1/

Liggio, C. D. (1974). The expectation gap: The accountant's Waterloo. *Journal of Contemporary Business, 3*, 27–44.

Llewellyn, S., & Milne, M. J. (2007). Accounting as codified discourse. *Accounting, Auditing & Accountability Journal, 20*(6), 805–824.

Lombardi, D. R., Bloch, R., & Vasarhelyi, M. A. (2015). The current state and future of the audit. *Current Issues in Auditing*, *9*(1), P10–P27.

Loscher, G. J., & Kaiser, S. (2020). The management of accounting firms: Time as an object of professional and commercial goals. *Journal of Accounting & Organizational Change*, *16*(1), 71–92.

MacDonald, E. (2006). *Where were the auditors?* Forbes.com.

Mackie, A. (2018, July 18). In defence of auditors: Detecting fraud is not their main job – But that could change. *Business Day*. https://www.businesslive.co.za/bd/opinion/2018-07-18-bridge-expectation-gap-with-a-new-consensus-on-audits/

Maguire, S., Hardy, C., & Lawrence, T. (2004). Institutional entrepreneurship in emerging fields: HIV/AIDS treatment advocacy in Canada. *Academy of Management Journal*, *47*(5), 657–679.

Makkawi, B., & Schick, A. (2003). Are auditors sensitive enough to fraud? *Managerial Auditing Journal*, *18*(6/7), 591–598.

Malsch, B., & O'Dwyer, B. (2021). New directions in auditing research: Conceptual repair, technological disruption (s), local professional governance and the battle for inclusivity. *European Accounting Review*, *30*(3), 439–444.

Marriage, M., & Martin, K. (2017). Watchdog admits it was slow to investigate HBOS audit. *The Financial Times*. https://www.ft.com/content/484265bc-d5cb-11e7-8c9a-d9c0a5c8d5c9

Marriage, M., & Rutter-Pooley, C. (2017). Review recommends larger fines for accountancy firms. *The Financial Times*. https://www.ft.com/content/60538b1e-ceae-11e7-9dbb-291a884dd8c6

Martin, M. (2023, April 25). The biggest financial fraud cases and Ponzi schemes in history. *Caseware*. https://www.caseware.com/ca/resources/blog/biggest-financial-fraud-cases-ponzi-schemes-history/#:~:text=As%20some%20of%20the%20cases,for%20their%20decisions%20and%20actions

Mason, L. (2024). The looming crisis: Shortage of audit candidates in the recruitment market. *IPS Finance*. https://www.ipsfinance.com/2024/05/02/the-looming-crisis-shortage-of-audit-candidates-in-the-recruitment-market/

Masters, B. (2018, January 5). PwC's failure to spot Colonial fraud spells trouble for auditors. *The Financial Times*. https://www.ft.com/content/c2cc45d6-f1f6-11e7-b220-857e26d1aca4

Matthews, D. (2006a). *A history of auditing: The changing audit process in Britain from the nineteenth century to the present day*. Routledge.

Matthews, D. (2006b). From ticking to clicking: Changes in auditing techniques in Britain from the 19th century to the present. *Accounting Historians Journal*, *33*(2), 63–102.

Maurer, M. (2023, September 22). Job security isn't enough to keep many accountants from quitting. *The Wall Street Journal*. https://www.wsj.com/articles/accounting-quit-job-security-675fc28f

Maurer, M. (2024, April 29). Auditors balk at regulator's push to expand their role. *The Wall Street Journal*. https://www.wsj.com/articles/auditors-balk-at-regulators-push-to-expand-their-role-fce0e030?mod=Searchresults_pos5&page=1

Mayorga, D. (2013). Managing continuous disclosure: Australian evidence. *Accounting, Auditing & Accountability Journal*, *26*(7), 1135–1169.

Mayston, D. (1993). Principals, agents and the economics of accountability in the new public sector. *Accounting, Auditing & Accountability Journal*, *6*(3), 68–96.

McCann, D. (2024, April 3). 71% of Big 4 auditors worry about mental health. *CFO*. https://www.cfo.com/news/71-of-big-4-auditors-worry-about-mental-health/712063/

McKenna, F. (2020). Weakening the oversight of US auditing is a very bad idea. *The Financial Times*. https://www.ft.com/content/efa3f33e-5170-11ea-a1ef-da1721a0541e

Meuwissen, R. (2014). The auditing profession. In K. Hay & J. Willekens (Eds.), *The Routledge companion to auditing* (pp. 17–38). Routledge.

Meyer, A. D., Brooks, G. R., & Goes, J. B. (1990). Environmental jolts and industry revolutions: Organizational responses to discontinuous change. *Strategic Management Journal*, *11*, 93–110.

Michael, A., & Dixon, R. (2019). Audit data analytics of unregulated voluntary disclosures and auditing expectations gap. *International Journal of Disclosure and Governance, 16*, 188–205.

Mikalef, P., van de Wetering, R., & Krogstie, J. (2021). Building dynamic capabilities by leveraging big data analytics: The role of organizational inertia. *Information & Management, 58*(6), 103412.

Millspaugh, P. E. (1995). The supreme court and state restraints on CPA business solicitation. *Akron Tax Journal, 11*, Article 3.

Mitchelmore, K. (2016). *The role of legacy in implementing change in long standing organizations: A case study* [a doctoral dissertation, faculty of business]. Athabasca.

Mo Koo, C., & Seog Sim, H. (1999). On the role conflict of auditors in Korea. *Accounting, Auditing & Accountability Journal, 12*(2), 206–219.

Mock, T. J., Bédard, J., Coram, P. J., Davis, S. M., Espahbodi, R., & Warne, R. C. (2013). The audit reporting model: Current research synthesis and implications. *Auditing: A Journal of Practice & Theory, 32*(sp1), 323–351.

Moffitt, K. C., Rozario, A. M., & Vasarhelyi, M. A. (2018). Robotic process automation for auditing. *Journal of Emerging Technologies in Accounting, 15*(1), 1–10.

Monroe, G. S., & Woodliff, D. R. (1993). The effect of education on the audit expectation gap. *Accounting & Finance, 33*(1), 61–78.

Moore, D. A., Tanlu, L., & Bazerman, M. H. (2010). Conflict of interest and the intrusion of bias. *Judgment and Decision Making, 5*(1), 37–53.

Moore, D. A., Tetlock, P. E., Tanlu, L., & Bazerman, M. H. (2006). Conflicts of interest and the case of auditor independence: Moral seduction and strategic issue cycling. *Academy of Management Review, 31*(1), 10–29.

Mouillon, C. (2018, June 25). Auditors need a stronger incentive to stand up to clients. *The Financial Times.* https://www.ft.com/content/ade02bfa-755f-11e8-bab2-43bd4ae655dd

Munck af Rosenschöld, J., Rozema, J. G., & Frye-Levine, L. A. (2014). Institutional inertia and climate change: A review of the new

# References

institutionalist literature. *Wiley Interdisciplinary Reviews: Climate Change*, 5(5), 639–648.

Noghondari, A. T., & Foong, S. Y. (2009). Audit expectation gap and loan decision performance of bank officers in Iran. *International Journal of Accounting, Auditing and Performance Evaluation*, 5(3), 310–328.

Nørreklit, H., Nørreklit, L., & Mitchell, F. (2010). Towards a paradigmatic foundation for accounting practice. *Accounting, Auditing & Accountability Journal*, 23(6), 733–758.

Nouri, H., & Parker, R. J. (2020). Turnover in public accounting firms: A literature review. *Managerial Auditing Journal*, 35(2), 294–321.

O'Dwyer, M. (2021, November 16). UK accounting watchdog tells Big Four to run businesses better. *The Financial Times*. https://www.ft.com/content/c8b1fe3d-d540-48ca-b5bf-e85134767061

O'Dwyer, M. (2022, December 8). Audit reform should not dance to the Big Four's tune. *The Financial Times*. https://www.ft.com/content/bb1a5605-48a7-47b5-be67-4d9f403b60fa

O'Dwyer, M. (2023, April 10). Smaller accounting firms ask Big Four to share their expertise. *The Financial Times*. https://www.ft.com/content/4605795a-e5c2-4033-be0d-e4caa3405a8c

Öhman, P., Häckner, E., Jansson, A. M., & Tschudi, F. (2006). Swedish auditors' view of auditing: Doing things right versus doing the right things. *European Accounting Review*, 15(1), 89–114.

Okike, E. (2004). Management of crisis: The response of the auditing profession in Nigeria to the challenge to its legitimacy. *Accounting, Auditing & Accountability Journal*, 17(5), 705–730.

Oliver, J. (2018, March 27). How to fix the Big Four auditors. *The Financial Times*. https://www.ft.com/content/2e840d7a-30ec-11e8-b5bf-23cb17fd1498

Olympics. (n.d.). *Deloitte, worldwide Olympic partner*. International Olympic Committee. https://olympics.com/ioc/partners/deloitte

Omodero, C. O., & Okafor, M. C. (2020). Audit education as an effective tool for narrowing audit Expectation gap: Evidence from literature review. *Journal of Educational and Social Research*, 10(5), 240–240.

Omoteso, K. (2012). The application of artificial intelligence in auditing: Looking back to the future. *Expert Systems with Applications, 39*(9), 8490–8495.

O'Reilly, D. M., Reisch, J. T., & Leitch, R. A. (2017). Do experienced auditors have a bias for confirmatory audit evidence? *International Journal of Accounting, Auditing and Performance Evaluation, 13*(2), 187–198.

PCAOB. (2012). *PCAOB announces settled disciplinary order for audit failures against Ernst & Young and four of its partners*. The Public Company Accounting Oversight Board. https://pcaobus.org/news-events/news-releases/news-release-detail/pcaob-announces-settled-disciplinary-order-for-audit-failures-against-ernst-young-and-four-of-its-partners_375

PCAOB. (2015, July 1). *Concept release on audit quality indicators*. The Public Company Accounting Oversight Board, PCAOB Release No. 2015-005. https://assets.pcaobus.org/pcaob-dev/docs/default-source/rulemaking/docket_041/release_2015_005.pdf?sfvrsn=de838d9f_0

Pereira, V. C., Pereira, A. G., & Oliveira, J. S. C. (2023). Influence of ownership structure on the choice of Big Four independent auditors. *International Journal of Disclosure and Governance, 20*(3), 316–326.

Picard, C. F. (2016). The marketization of accountancy. *Critical Perspectives on Accounting, 34*, 79–97.

Picard, C. F., Durocher, S., & Gendron, Y. (2014). From meticulous professionals to superheroes of the business world: A historical portrait of a cultural change in the field of accountancy. *Accounting, Auditing & Accountability Journal, 27*(1), 73–118.

Pickard, J., & Naumenko, S. (2024). World survey supplement: Growth remains positive for top accountancy networks and associations. *GlobalData*. https://accounting.h5mag.com/iab_ws24_supplement/growth_remains_positive_for_top_accountancy_networks_and_associations

Pierce, B., & Sweeney, B. (2004). Cost–quality conflict in audit firms: An empirical investigation. *European Accounting Review, 13*(3), 415–441.

Ponomareva, Y., Uman, T., Broberg, P., Vinberg, E., & Karlsson, K. (2020). Commercialization of audit firms and auditors' subjective well-being. *Meditari Accountancy Research, 28*(4), 565–585.

Porter, B. (1993). An empirical study of the audit expectation-performance gap. *Accounting and Business Research*, 24(93), 49–68.

Porter, M. E. (2008). The five competitive forces that shape strategy. *Harvard Business Review*, 86(1), 78.

PTI. (2018, June 3). Auditors step up pressure on listed firms, start flagging gaps. *ET Markets*. https://economictimes.indiatimes.com/markets/stocks/news/auditors-step-up-pressure-on-listed-clients-start-flagging-gaps/articleshow/64435976.cms

PWC. (2000). *Letter to the secretary of the U.S. securities and exchange commission.* https://www.sec.gov/rules/proposed/s71300/pricewa1.htm

Quick, R. (2020). The audit expectation gap: A review of the academic literature. *Maandblad Voor Accountancy en Bedrijfseconomie*, 94(1/2), 5–25.

Ramanna, K. (2019). Building a culture of challenge in audit firms, a paper commissioned by PwC UK as part of the future of audit initiative. *PwC*. https://www.pwc.co.uk/who-we-are/future-of-audit/building-a-culture-of-challenge-in-audit-firms.pdf

Ramirez, C. (2012). How Big Four audit firms control standard-setting in accounting and auditing. In *Finance: The discreet regulator: How financial activities shape and transform the world* (pp. 40–58). Palgrave Macmillan UK.

Rasyid, A. (2013). Relevance of Islamic dispute resolution processes in Islamic banking and finance. *Arab Law Quarterly*, 27(4), 343–369.

Reddit. (n.d.). *Do you believe that audit work is undervalued or overvalued?* https://www.reddit.com/r/Accounting/comments/njoyfw/do_you_believe_that_audit_work_is_undervalued_or/

Reffett, A., Brewster, B. E., & Ballou, B. (2012). Comparing auditor versus non-auditor assessments of auditor liability: An experimental investigation of experts' versus lay evaluators' judgments. *Auditing: A Journal of Practice & Theory*, 31(3), 125–148.

Rennie, M. D., Kopp, L. S., & Lemon, W. M. (2010). Exploring trust and the auditor-client relationship: Factors influencing the auditor's trust of a client representative. *Auditing: A Journal of Practice & Theory*, 29(1), 279–293.

Richard, P. J. (2008, October 10). Where were auditors as companies collapsed? *American Banker*. https://www.americanbanker.com/news/viewpoint-where-were-auditors-as-companies-collapsed

Richardson, A. (2017). The accountancy profession. *The Routledge companion to critical accounting* (pp. 127–142).

Richardson, P., Dellaportas, S., Perera, L., & Richardson, B. (2015). Towards a conceptual framework on the categorization of stereotypical perceptions in accounting. *Journal of Accounting Literature*, 35(1), 28–46.

Ronen, J. (2010). Corporate audits and how to fix them. *Journal of Economic Perspectives*, 24(2), 189–210.

Rosenbaum, E. (2022). Mental models and institutional inertia. *Journal of Institutional Economics*, 18(3), 361–378.

Rosenschöld, J., Rozema, J. G., & Frye-Levine, L. A. (2014). Institutional inertia and climate change: A review of the new institutionalist literature. *Wiley Interdisciplinary Reviews: Climate Change*, 5(5), 639–648.

RSM Global. (n.d.). https://www.rsm.global/malta/news/rsm-malta-sponsors-shark-tank-third-consecutive-season

Ruhnke, K., & Schmidt, M. (2014). The audit expectation gap: Existence, causes, and the impact of changes. *Accounting and Business Research*, 44(5), 572–601.

Ruhnke, K., & Schmitz, S. (2019). Review engagements–structure of audit firm methodology and its situational application in Germany. *Journal of International Accounting, Auditing and Taxation*, 37, 100289.

Ruiz Castro, M. (2012). Time demands and gender roles: The case of a big four firm in Mexico. *Gender, Work & Organization*, 19(5), 532–554.

Salijeni, G., Samsonova-Taddei, A., & Turley, S. (2021). Understanding how big data technologies reconfigure the nature and organization of financial statement audits: A sociomaterial analysis. *European Accounting Review*, 30(3), 531–555.

Schelluch, P., & Gay, G. (2006). Assurance provided by auditors' reports on prospective financial information: implications for the expectation gap. Accounting & Finance, 46(4), 653–676.

# References

Schmitt, C., Henry, N., & Arondekar, A. (2002). Introduction: Victorian investments. *Victorian Studies*, 45(1), 7–16.

Scott, W. R. (2003). Institutional carriers: Reviewing modes of transporting ideas over time and space and considering their consequences. *Industrial and Corporate Change*, 12(4), 879–894.

Securities and Exchange Commission (SEC). (2000, July 26). *United States securities & exchange commission hearing on auditor independence*. https://www.sec.gov/files/rules/extra/audmin.htm

Shah, A., & Grimstone, G. (2019). Do the CMA auditing proposals make sense? *The Financial Times*. https://www.ft.com/content/c9c4bf50-61d3-11e9-9300-0becfc937c37

Sidani, Y. (2023). How business schools can graduate business citizens. In A. Örtenblad & R. Koris (Eds.), *Debating business school legitimacy: Attacking, rocking, and defending the status quo* (pp. 217–233). Springer International Publishing.

Sidani, Y., & Al Ariss, A. (2014). Institutional and corporate drivers of global talent management: Evidence from the Arab Gulf region. *Journal of World Business*, 49(2), 215–224.

Siew, S. (2018, October 8). *The truth about work-life balance at a Big Four*. Women in Business at Indiana University. https://www.iuwib.com/blog/

Sikka, P. (2008). Enterprise culture and accountancy firms: New masters of the universe. *Accounting, Auditing & Accountability Journal*, 21(2), 268–295.

Sikka, P., Filling, S., & Liew, P. (2009). The audit crunch: Reforming auditing. *Managerial Auditing Journal*, 24(2), 135–155.

Sioˆn Owen, A. (2003). Measuring large UK accounting firm profit margins, mergers and concentration: A political economy of the accounting firm. *Accounting, Auditing & Accountability Journal*, 16(2), 275–297.

Smieliauskas, W., Ye, M., & Zhang, P. (2020). *Auditing and society: Research on audit practice and regulations*. Routledge.

Smith, H. L. (1958). Contingencies of professional differentiation. *American Journal of Sociology*, 63(4), 410–414.

Smolinski, H. C., Chumley, D. W., & Bennett, D. E. (1992). In search of ancient auditors. *Accounting Historians Notebook*, 15(2), 7–26.

Sori, Z. M., Karbhari, Y., & Mohamad, S. (2010). Commercialization of the accounting profession: The case of non-audit services. *International Journal of Economics and Management*, 4(2), 212–242.

Spence, C., & Carter, C. (2014). An exploration of the professional habitus in the Big 4 accounting firms. *Work, Employment and Society*, 28(6), 946–962.

Stevens, E., Moroney, R., & Webster, J. (2019). Professional skepticism: The combined effect of partner style and team identity salience. *International Journal of Auditing*, 23(2), 279–291.

Suchman, M. C. (1995). Managing legitimacy: Strategic and institutional approaches. *Academy of Management Review*, 20(3), 571–610.

Suddaby, R., Gendron, Y., & Lam, H. (2009). The organizational context of professionalism in accounting. *Accounting, Organizations and Society*, 34(3–4), 409–427.

Tadros, E. (2023, October 23). Unpleasant work or low pay? What's behind the auditor shortage. *Financial Review*. https://www.afr.com/companies/professional-services/unpleasant-work-or-low-pay-what-s-behind-the-auditor-shortage-20231022-p5ee3o

Talar, S. (2012). 382 Introducing the muḥtasib. In K. Stilt (Ed.), *Islamic law in action: Authority, discretion, and everyday experiences in Mamluk Egypt*. Oxford University Press.

Tantawy, S. M., & Moussa, T. (2023). The effect of political connections on firms' auditor choice decisions and audit opinions: Evidence from Egypt. *Asian Review of Accounting*, 31(3), 414–436.

Teal HQ. (n.d.). Auditor skills in 2025 (Top + most underrated skills). *Teal HQ*. https://www.tealhq.com/skills/auditor

Teo, E. J., & Cobbin, P. E. (2005). A revisitation of the "audit expectations gap": Judicial and practitioner views on the role of the auditor in late-Victorian England. *Accounting History*, 10(2), 35–66.

The Economist. (2003, February 13). Auditing the auditors: An ex-PricewaterhouseCoopers man tilts at the Big Four. *The Economist*.

https://www.economist.com/finance-and-economics/2003/02/13/auditing-the-auditors

The Economist. (2017, December 14). Who audits the auditors? America's Public Company accounting oversight board gets a new boss. *The Economist*. https://www.economist.com/business/2017/12/14/americas-public-company-accounting-oversight-board-gets-a-new-boss

The Economist. (2018a, May 24). Shape up, not break up: Reforming the Big Four. *The Economist*. https://www.economist.com/leaders/2018/05/24/reforming-the-big-four

The Economist. (2018b, May 26). The great expectations gap: What is an audit for? *The Economist*. https://www.economist.com/finance-and-economics/2018/05/26/what-is-an-audit-for

Thomas, H. (2018, May 21). Carillion: The audit industry's existential question. *BBC*. https://www.bbc.com/news/business-44201251

Thomas, H. (2021, September 27). UK audit failings highlight need for new approach. *The Financial Times*. https://www.ft.com/content/cf5153c6-52bb-43dd-9efd-817aeaf7bb93

Thomson Reuters Tax & Accounting. (2024). *The future of audit talent*. https://tax.thomsonreuters.com/blog/the-future-of-audit-talent/

Thomson Reuters Tax & Accounting. (2024, September 30). From the auditor's perspective: What does the future of the audit profession look like? *Thomson Reuters*. https://tax.thomsonreuters.com/blog/from-the-auditors-perspective-what-does-the-future-of-the-audit-profession-look-like/

Thornton, P. H., & Ocasio, W. (1999). Institutional logics and the historical contingency of power in organizations: Executive succession in the higher education publishing industry, 1958–1990. *American Journal of Sociology*, *105*(3), 801–843.

Thornton, P. H., Jones, C., & Kury, K. (2005). Institutional logics and institutional change in organizations: Transformation in accounting, architecture, and publishing. C. Jones & P. H. Thornton (Eds.), *Transformation in cultural industries (research in the sociology of organizations*, Vol. 23, pp. 125–170). Emerald Group Publishing Limited.

Thornton, P. H., Ocasio, W., & Lounsbury, M. (2012). *The institutional logics perspective: A new approach to culture, structure, and process.* Oxford University Press on Demand.

Tiberius, V., & Hirth, S. (2019). Impacts of digitization on auditing: A Delphi study for Germany. *Journal of International Accounting, Auditing and Taxation, 37,* 100288.

Tolleson, T. D., & Pai, K. (2011). The big 4 accounting firms: Too big to fail? *International Journal of Business, Accounting & Finance, 5*(1), 56–66.

Tomo, A., & Spanò, R. (2020). Strategising identity in the accounting profession: "Mirror, mirror on the wall, who is the accountant of them all?" *Meditari Accountancy Research, 28*(6), 917–949.

Treviño, L. K., Weaver, G. R., Gibson, D. G., & Toffler, B. L. (1999). Managing ethics and legal compliance: What works and what hurts. *California Management Review, 41*(2), 131–151.

Trinkle, B. S., Warkentin, M., Malimage, K., & Raddatz, N. (2021). High-risk deviant decisions: Does neutralization still play a role? *Journal of the Association for Information Systems, 22*(3), 3.

Trullion. (2024, January 2). The future of auditing: Trends to watch in 2024. *Trullion.* https://trullion.com/blog/the-future-of-auditing-trends-to-watch-in-2024/

Tyler, T., Dienhart, J., & Thomas, T. (2008). The ethical commitment to compliance: Building value-based cultures. *California Management Review, 50*(2), 31–51.

Vanasco, R. R. (1998). Fraud auditing. *Managerial Auditing Journal, 13*(1), 4–71.

Warmoll, C. (2013, April 16). Grant Thornton wins Parmalat audit legal spat. *Business & Accountancy Daily.* https://www.accountancydaily.co/grant-thornton-wins-parmalat-audit-legal-spat

Wedlin, L. (2008). University marketization: The process and its limits. In L. Engwall & D. Weaire (Eds.), *The university in the market* (Vol. 84, pp. 143–153), London: Portland Press.

Whittle, A., Mueller, F., & Carter, C. (2016). The 'Big Four'in the spotlight: Accountability and professional legitimacy in the UK audit market. *Journal of Professions and Organization, 3*(2), 119–141.

Wijaya, A., Suryani, B., Pratama, C., Permadi, D., & Putri, E. (2021). Auditors' perception on ethical responsibility in auditing: A qualitative study. *Golden Ratio of Auditing Research, 1*(1), 01–10.

Williams, E. Y. (2023, November 7). *PCAOB Chair Williams delivers remarks at international institute on audit regulation.* The Public Company Accounting Oversight Board. https://pcaobus.org/news-events/speeches/speech-detail/pcaob-chair-williams-delivers-remarks-at-international-institute-on-audit-regulation-2023

Willmott, H., & Sikka, P. (1997). On the commercialization of accountancy thesis: A review essay. *Accounting, Organizations and Society, 22*(8), 831–842.

Wilson, N. (2024, March 27). Underpaid, overworked: The audit profession's 'battle' for talent. *Accountants Daily.* https://www.accountantsdaily.com.au/business/19776-underpaid-overworked-the-audit-professions-battle-for-talent

Windsor, C., & Warming-Rasmussen, B. (2009). The rise of regulatory capitalism and the decline of auditor independence: A critical and experimental examination of auditors' conflicts of interests. *Critical Perspectives on Accounting, 20*(2), 267–288.

Wolf, F. M., Tackett, J. A., & Claypool, G. A. (1999). Audit disaster futures: Antidotes for the expectation gap? *Managerial Auditing Journal, 14*(9), 468–478.

Wood, T. D., & Sylvestre, A. J. (1985). The history of advertising by accountants. *The Accounting Historians Journal, 12*(2), 59–72.

Woolf, A. H. (1912). *A short history of accountants and accountancy.* Gee.

Wyatt, A. R. (2004). Accounting professionalism-They just don't get it! *Accounting Horizons, 18*(1), 45–54.

Yapa, P. W. S., Ukwatte Jalathge, S. L., & Siriwardhane, P. (2017). The professionalisation of auditing in less developed countries: The case of Sri Lanka. *Managerial Auditing Journal, 32*(4/5), 500–523.

Yuen, C. K., Pan, G., & Goh, C. (2020). *Audit profession must rid 'overworked, underpaid' image to attract best talent* (pp. 1–3). HRM Asia. https://ink.library.smu.edu.sg/soa_research/1905

Zakiyah, N., Prananingtyas, P., Disemadi, H. S., & Gubanov, K. (2019). Al-Hisbah contextualization in the business competition law in Indonesia. *Al-'Adalah*, *16*(2), 249–262.

Zhang, P. (2007). The impact of the public's expectations of auditors on audit quality and auditing standards compliance. *Contemporary Accounting Research*, *24*(2), 631–654.

# INDEX

Acceptance (A), 85
Accountability, 3–4, 5, 28, 32
Accountancy, 38, 49
Accountant(s), 57–59
   accountant-entrepreneur, 57
   guardian, 57
   identity, 56–57
Accounting
   adapting to accounting
      principles, 73–74
   firms, 42–44, 46, 49, 52, 63
   industry, 48
   practitioners and scholars, 11
   profession, 42, 44, 69
   professionalism, 41
   professionals, 17
   services, 47
   stereotype, 69–70
   trainees, 69
Accreditation agencies, 82
Active conspirators, 37
Additional services, 53
Adhocracy culture, 43
Advertising, 48
Agility (A), 79
Agility, competence, ethical
      grounding & character
      (ACE), 78–80
Alignment with industry (A), 82
American Accounting
      Association, 42
American Association of Public
      Accountants
      (AAPA), 47–48
American Institute of Accountants, 7
American Institute of Certified
      Public Accountants
      (AICPA), 7, 38, 45, 65

Anchoring bias, 22
Arthur Andersen, 10, 34, 52, 64
Artificial intelligence (AI), 18, 71, 73
Association of Chartered Certified
      Accountants (ACCA),
      18, 27–28
Association to Advance Collegiate
      Schools of Business
      (AACSB), 83
Assurance services, 41
Attractiveness, 55
"Audit", 3, 29
   audit-by-exception, 73
   audit–client relationship, 21
   committees, 2, 23
   embracing change in audit
      profession, 70–71
   engagement, 34
   expectations gap, 2, 36, 77, 85
   failures, 25, 52, 55, 58
   firms, 51, 67
   function, 33
   independence, 2, 12
   industry, 38
   information, 36
   profession, 17, 64, 77
   quality, 16–17, 29, 33
   reform, 20
   reports, 11
   techniques, 10
   work, 34
Auditing, 4, 52
   20th century and on, 9–12
   adapting to new accounting
      principles, 73–74
   addressing auditor
      responsibilities in fraud
      detection, 71

auditor independence, 21–24
boards, 38
challenges, 12–13
embracing change in audit profession, 70–71
embracing new mindset in, 65–66
expanding assurance services beyond financial information, 72
expectations gap, 37
field of, 66
firms, 34
fraud detection, 13–15
function, 7
growth of profession, 6–9
history, 3–5
identity, 55–59
leveraging technology for comprehensive audits, 72–73
medieval auditing practices, 5–6
nature of, 26
oligarchy, 19–21
organizational cultures, 43–46
overcoming institutional inertia, 74
profession, 1–3, 12, 15–16, 25, 61, 65, 68, 79
professional logics *vs.* market logics, 46–55
professionals, 17
redefining, 70
services, 27, 47
shift toward real-time auditing, 71–72
smarter, 14
talent attraction and retention, 15–19
Auditor(s), 13, 30, 32–33, 38, 53–54, 62, 72, 80
independence, 21–24
liability, 28
maintaining, 21
report, 32
responsibility of, 36
role of, 13, 36
struggle, 21
technology skills, 77
Availability bias, 22

Bates v. State Bar of Arizona, 48
BDO, 50
Bean counter, 56, 70
Behavioral inertia, 62–63
*Beit-ul-Mal* (Treasury), 4
Bias, 22, 62
Big accounting firms, 41–42, 71, 74
much-maligned dominance, 67
role of, 66–67
Big Eight firms, 45
Big Five accounting, 34
Big Four, 20, 67, 70
accounting, 11–12, 19
accounting firms, 23, 25, 44, 46, 49
auditors, 32, 58
firms, 18, 20
function, 63
governance issues, 19
revenues, 19
Boring bookkeeper, 70
Brexit, 16
Building relationships (B), 84
Business(es), 6
acumen, 49
environment, 85
firms, 82
schools of, 80–83

Capitalistic society, 48
Certified Public Accountant (CPA), 8, 17
Character & ethics development (C), 82
Chartered accountant, 8
Clan culture, 43
Client welfare, 49
Climate change issues, 72
Codes of conduct, 45
Cognitive legitimacy, 52
Cohen Commission of auditors, 2
Collective dominance, 20
Colorful accountant, 58, 70
Colorful identity, 58
Commercial identity, 58
Commercial logics, 48–52
Commercialism, 52, 54, 67

# Index

Commercialization, 49, 51
   in accounting, 54
   legitimizing, 52–55
Communication (C), 85–86
Companies Act, 8–9
Competence (C), 79–80
Competing Values Framework (CVF), 43
Comprehensive audits, leveraging technology for, 72–73
Comprehensive fraud prevention, 15
Computer
   computer-aided auditing, 12
   technology, 42
Confirmation bias, 22
Cooper, W., 7
Corporate failures, 25, 32
Corporate mismanagement, 32
Cost–benefit considerations, 36
Credibility, impact on, 39
Criticism, 20
Critics, 29
Culture reviews, 19
Customer centricity, 52–53
Customer satisfaction, 53
Cybersecurity risks, 72

Data analysis, 12
Data analytics (DA), 71
Deloitte, W., 7, 19, 23, 37
*Dewan*, 4
Double culture, 54
Dynamism, 55

Education of accountants, 57
Educational institutions, 80–83
Educational programs, 82
Employees, 16
Enhanced financial disclosures, 11
Enron, 34, 45, 51–52, 64
Entrepreneur identity, 58
Environmental, Social, and Governance (ESG), 51, 72, 80
Environmental auditing, 72
Ethical grounding & character (E), 80
Ethical practice (E), 83–84

Ethical Practice, Mentorship, Building Relationships, Responsiveness, Acceptance, Communication, Excellence (EMBRACE), 78, 83–86
Ethics education, 82
Evergrande, 34
Evolution gap, 29
Excellence (E), 85
Exceptional exceptions, 73
Expectations gap, 27–32, 37, 77, 85
   causes of, 32
   conflicts at levels, 37–38
   impact on reputation and credibility, 39
   increased litigation risk, 37
   lobbying and overregulation, 38–39
   outcomes of, 37
   performance deficiencies, 34–35
   public perceptions and, 36
   self-regulation and professional evolution, 32–33
   standards and regulatory frameworks, 35
Experiential & lifelong learning (E), 83
Experiential learning, 83
EY, 38

Federal Deposit Insurance Corporation (FDIC), 1
Fibonacci, L., 5
Financial crash (1929), 45
Financial information, expanding assurance services beyond, 72
Financial Reporting Council (FRC), 11
Financial statements, 1, 3, 28, 36
Financial system, 17
*Financial Times*, 2, 19–20, 25, 33
Firms, 49
Flag possible fraud, 13

Fraud, 30
    addressing auditor responsibilities in fraud detection, 71
    detection, 13–15, 32
    fraud-risk assessment performance, 15
    prevention, 4, 14, 24, 30
Full population testing, 73

Global Data World Survey, 19
Gradual process of marketization, 50
Grandiosity, 43
Grant Thornton, 37
Groupthink, 22
Guarantor against fraud, 13

Healthcare industry, 54
Henry I, 5
Henry II, 5
Hierarchy culture, 43
High-profile audit failures or allegations, 39
High-quality audits, 54
*Hisbah*, 4
Human resources, 16

Identity, 55–56
    accountant identity, 56–57
    crisis, 59
    identity crises and reconstruction, 59
    and professionalism, 57
    reconstruction, 68
    risks of stereotype shifts, 57–59
Independence, 21, 23, 52
Industrial revolution, 6
Inertia, 70
Information asymmetry, 36, 39
Institute of Chartered Accountants in England and Wales (ICAEW), 8
Institutional entrepreneurs, 3, 69
Institutional entrepreneurship
    changing accounting stereotype, 69–70
    evolution of professional accountant's image, 68–69
    identity reconstruction, 68
    return to professionalism, 67–68
    role of, 66
    role of big accounting firms, 66–67
    role of institutional entrepreneurs, 69
Institutional inertia, 62
    behavioral inertia and path dependence, 62–63
    embracing new mindset in auditing, 65–66
    factors contributing to institutional inertia, 61–62
    lobbying and regulatory influence, 64–65
    overcoming, 74
    resistance to change and status quo, 63–64
    impact of scandals and self-regulation, 64
Institutional logics, 46
Institutional maintenance, 63
Institutional transformation, 63
Institutions, 61
International Federation of Accountants (IFAC), 10
International Financial Reporting Standards (IFRS), 10
International Forum of Independent Audit Regulators, 34
International Standards on Auditing (ISAs), 11

Job security, 16

Kingston Cotton Mill Decision, 8
Knowledge gap, 28
KPMG, 37

Large accounting firms, 12, 20, 46, 50, 64–65, 70
Leadership skills (L), 82
Leading accounting, 17
Legal liability, 23

# Index

Legislative bodies, 72
Legitimacy, 58, 66, 85
Legitimation, 53
Litigation risk, increased, 37
Lobbying, 38–39, 64–65
Logic equilibrium, 68

Machine learning, 73
Making audit, 63
Market
  culture, 43
  leadership, 49
  orientation, 51
  market-oriented approach, 8
Market logics, 46–47
  commercial logics, 48–52
  legitimizing commercialization, 52–55
  professional logics, 47–48
Marketing expertise, 50
Marketization, 49–50
Media
  bias against auditors, 39
  representatives, 28
Medicis Pharmaceutical Corporation, 34
Medieval auditing practices, 5–6
Mental models, 62
Mentorship (M), 84
Migration regulations, 16
Modern auditing profession, 7, 9
*Muhtasib*, 4–5

Non-audit services, 19, 22, 25, 45, 51

Old auditing, 53
Omar Ibn El Khattab, 4
Operational audit, 5
Ordre des comptables agréés du Québec (OCAQ), 49
Organizational cultures, 43–46
Overregulation, 38–39

Pacioli's bookkeeping method, 6
Parmalat, 37
Path dependence, 62–63

Peat, W. B., 7
Performance deficiencies, 34–35
Performance gap, 28
Performance pressures, 51
Personal authorization, 52
"Poaching", 16
Practice codes, 34
Price, S. L., 7
Profession, growth of, 6–9
Professional accountant's image, evolution of, 68–69
Professional auditor, 3, 6, 52, 68, 73
Professional development (P), 81
Professional development, Leadership skills, Alignment with industry, Character & ethics development, Experiential & lifelong learning (PLACE), 78, 80–83
Professional evolution, 32–33
Professional logics, 46–48
  commercial logics, 48–52
  legitimizing commercialization, 52–55
Professional organizations, 74
Professional skepticism, 13
Professional standards, 34
Professional transformation, 55
Professionalism, 54, 67
  identity and, 57
  return to, 67–68
Professionalization, 12, 68
Public accountants, 54
Public accounting, 47
Public Company Accounting Oversight Board (PCAOB), 11, 13, 38–39, 64
Public interest entities (PIEs), 22
Public perceptions, 36
"Public recognition" of accountants, 7
Purchased service, 26
PwC, 32, 38, 70
PwC China, 34

Quaestors, 4

Rationalization, instrumental, 53
Rationalization, theoretical, 52
Real-time auditing, shift toward, 71–72
Reasonableness gap, 36
Regulatory influence, 64–65
Reimagining auditing, 78–79, 84
Reputation, impact on, 39
Resistance to change, 63–64
Responsiveness (R), 84–85
Risk-based auditing, 12
RSM international, 50

Sarbanes-Oxley Act (2002), 11, 45
Scandals, impact of, 64
Schools of business, 80–83
Scorekeeper, 56
Secondhand affective reactions, 23
Securities Act (1933), 9
Securities and Exchange Act (1934), 9
Securities and Exchange Commission (SEC), 9, 38
Securities Exchange Act (1934), 9, 11, 38
Selective perception, 22
Self-interested profession, 32–33

Self-regulating monopoly, 65
Self-regulation, 32–33, 45, 64
Self-serving bias, 23
Smith report, 11
Stakeholders, 2, 25–26, 30, 34, 39, 72, 77
    causes of expectations gap, 32–36
    expectations gap, 27–32
    outcomes of expectations gap, 37–39
Stereotype shifts, risks of, 57–59
Sustainability, 72

Tacit Collusion, 20
Talent attraction and retention, 15–19
Talent shortage, 17
Technology, 18, 71
Tight oligopoly, 20
Trade networks, 5
Transnational epistemic community, 64
Treadway Commission, 13
Tripartite model, 78

UK Companies Act, The, 7

*Zakat*, 4

www.ingramcontent.com/pod-product-compliance
Lightning Source LLC
LaVergne TN
LVHW011604060925
820435LV00022B/207